Your Angels Are Speaking

Your Angels Are Speaking

Sharon Rahm, R.N., and Wendy Krause

Writers Club Press

San Jose New York Lincoln Shanghai

Your Angels Are Speaking

Writers Club Press
an imprint of iUniverse.com, Inc.

For information address:
iUniverse.com, Inc.
5220 S 16th, Ste. 200
Lincoln, NE 68512
www.iuniverse.com

ISBN: 0-595-14724-0

Printed in the United States of America

To Lois Smith and to Brandy

Preface

The new millennium is before us and always has been. We (the angels, spirit guides, archangels and ascended masters) will hold your hand and welcome you into a time of wonderful, positive, rewarding changes. God is with you every step. He will become more visible as the beings on Earth yearn to recognize, see and feel Him in every breath, relaxation and respite. You are reading this book because you not only want answers, but you want to change the way you feel. These words will guide you. They will encourage and push you to contact the universal wisdom of God as a part of your life. The best use of this information is problem solving, identifying and returning your attention to the perfect essence which is you.

Taking a break from the stresses of life can be a permanent way to live. We teach that on the planet Earth it is not the big things that are as stressful to you as the constant supply of small stresses and small fires to put out on a daily basis. You will feel a tremendous sense of relief, peace and relaxation when you decide and intend to turn problems over to the angels and to God. To clarify, God and the angels are one and it does not offend God for you to ask the angels for help. The angels stand ready to assist you in any matter. You have at least two guardian angels that stand by you your entire life to assist you at your request. They do not interfere unless asked for their help. No matter is too small or too big. Do you not feel great on the days that such a small thing as finding a good parking place occurs? Yes, these are the angels assisting you and directing you to the vacant spot. Multiply this good feeling by many deeds turning out well each day and you will continue to relax into the life of angel assistance.

Let us inform you of the ways you will receive guidance and assistance and suggestions from your angels. First, you may picture or see in your mind's eye a solution. Secondly, you may hear a little voice giving you information. Thirdly, you may have a hunch or gut feeling that guides you. Or, fourthly, you may just "know" the answer to the problem. You may have a combination of several of these avenues of information occur simultaneously. Whichever or whatever happens, record in a journal or in your memory that it occurred and was successful for you. You then will trust these suggestions more often and experience more success and increase your feelings of well being.

This book will describe in detail how to talk to and reach out for help from these heavenly messengers who stand by ready for your call to assist you in every matter.

The help you have asked for is within these pages. This is why you have picked up this book.

Introduction

Your Angels Are Speaking was channeled through Sharon Rahm over a four-month period. Sharon received information from God and the angelic realm through automatic writing. For this book, Sharon was told what the topic would be and the text would follow. Sharon's sister, Wendy Krause, compiled and edited the material with only very minor changes to the text. These words from the angelic realm needed very little editing. In this pure form one can truly feel the impact of the angels' words, love and guidance.

This introduction is to clarify the necessity of these words. They are plain and simple and easy to understand and easy to follow. Read these words as you would a training manual or any other piece of material that you would read to improve your life and your lifestyle. This book will go further and will improve your life and your spirituality for all of your days. The words between these covers not only caress you and encourage you to go beyond your own dreams of power, but will inspire you to share these words and the love with all you meet!

We ask that you read each word and each chapter slowly and carefully digesting the meanings and allowing them truly to enter your soul and become a part of you. You will need to read and re-read the words as necessary to bring you back to your spiritual center and to love.

Keep this manual near you. It is your guide on how to live in this new millennium and how to do so with love and with grace. We, the authors, are proud and excited to offer up these words to you for your use. We, too, have a long journey ahead of us and need these words to guide us daily in our lightwork on this planet.

Mother Earth has been discussed herein so please reflect on what you can do in your town or in your neighborhood to beautify and cleanse her and touch her with love daily. She is your home, our home, and we must heed her calls and cries for help just as we would a crying child in the night.

Each of us has guardian angels and angels who come and go throughout our lifetime. Learn to listen and to trust them as you move through your days and your lives. Listen to their gentle and loving words and nudges to help you make the right choices. Be not afraid as you listen in wonderment and awe. They are only here for your highest good. They are only here for your protection on this Earth. They will never leave you. You are not alone and these words should comfort you and help you to understand that truth.

Sharon Rahm, R.N., and Wendy Krause

Table of Contents

Chapter 1

Remembering the Truth

The truth is that only love matters. God's love for you is unconditional. We are all one with God and God's omnipresence means that He is everywhere. Then He is in us and everyone else. We are all one with each other. There is nothing we could do or have done that changes God's love for us.

The truths:

> * Love is the basis for all.
> * God's love for you is unconditional.
> * You are on the planet to complete a mission.
> * You are on the planet with a set of goals to accomplish.
> * You have free will.
> * There is no death.
> * You are perfect, whole and complete.

The strengths to make it through the day start with these truths. God loves you unconditionally. There is nothing you have done or ever could do to change that. God is not a punishing God. He will assist you to correct your mistakes. You are perfect, whole and complete. You are made by God in this perfect way. The essence which is you is perfect, whole and complete.

Before you were born you set goals and expected accomplishments and challenges for this lifetime. You planned to share your life with certain others you have known in other lives. In the process of your life on this planet much has happened to hide your perfect self from you. Think of each challenge, stress and deed as having the effect of putting a layer of fabric around you. Soon you have many fabrics and a very thick shell. The real you which is love has not changed or diminished in any way. You need to take off this shell so you can live and do from a love basis which is you.

This shell is produced from fears you have had in this lifetime and other lifetimes. Releasing these fears which block your love from coming through to yourself and others can be done easily. Please do not think of this process as painful, difficult or time consuming. You will realize that it is not and you can relax and enjoy the results. We will show you how you can do this easily with the help of God and your angels. The result is a sense of love and well being like you may have never experienced before.

Your angels and guardian angels love you unconditionally, as does God. These angels stand by you your entire life waiting for you to ask them for help. Since there is the law of free will, you cannot receive angel help unless you ask for it. The angels do not have permission to intervene in your life unless it is a life-threatening situation. You will see that it is easy to ask the angels to assist you and to guide you. Your higher self is in touch with the universal wisdom of God. You have all of the answers inside of you and you will remember how to get in contact with this source.

This is a time to remind one of the ego self. The ego self drives you daily into its land of fear, anger and every other feeling which is not love. Ease out of these habits. The ego will pull you and drive you. The ego will argue with this material in order to drive away love and to give fear a home in which to grow. Where there is love ego and fear cannot reside.

We will show you how to know if it is a love or an ego-driven fear that resides in the base of the issue.

* Angel guidance comes from only love. Love is unconditional and accepting of all. Ego guidance as we have said comes from fear.
* Angel guidance makes you feel good about yourself and others. Ego-based feelings are frightening, negative and insight bad feelings. Ego feelings put oneself before all others.

* Angel guidance and love make you feel good, proud, joyous and excited to be alive. Ego-based thoughts and words make you feel bad, ashamed, sorry, and undeserving of anything good.
* Love feelings promote love for God and desire to reside in joy with Him. Ego-based thoughts tell you there is no God or that we have a punishing God. Thoughts like "If there really is a God he wouldn't let me suffer" are common feelings that the ego sends out.

This is a time for the world to unite with feelings of God's love and influence and the time to remove the ego from power in yourselves.

Not a Punishing God

So often you cringe in fear at the thought of God seeing your actions or hearing your words and feeling sorry and ashamed. "Boy, am I going to get it on judgment day." First, understand, dear one, that there is nothing you have done or ever could do to make God not love you or change his love for you in any way. His love is unconditional. God teaches that mistakes are to be corrected, not punished. There are other ways of releasing the negative effects of actions and thoughts. Often and too frequently, you choose to punish yourselves quickly and extremely. This is done at the direction of ego. This is not God's intervention. You are deserving of only love, not punishment. Allow this truth to settle in your heart and grow.

Chapter 2

Angels for Daily Life and Living

Angel Strength and Why We Need Angels

Today there are mighty forces at work which are the stresses of life on your planet. The daily struggles needn't be. The plan is to have the humans ask for, lean on, and call on us, your angels, for each and every situation. The inequities you think you have are not here.

When events occur you can choose how to react to them and this is the key of life. Choose the easy way. Choose the loving way. It is a frame of mind that you must realize that we are all one with each other and one with God. Choosing to come from love is the easy part. You must have help to make this happen or to manifest this attitude in your thoughts and speech.

The first concept to understand and re-learn is that God has made you perfect, whole and complete. You must realize and remember this. You must then shed the outer covering which is an artificial personality you have adopted on this earthly planet. No, this doesn't mean you're going to change drastically. It means that your love and true essence will guide and direct you in all things. This is an exciting plan as it leads to many benefits not only for you but also for others you encounter and with whom you share your life.

The essence knows all and is wise beyond imagination. Trusting this essence is something many of you need to re-learn. Yes, there is help to do that. This essence has been through many lives and, of course, has much experience. It is this essence who participated in the planning of your current life. Therefore, you have planned to attract events to you for your higher growth and advancement in your spiritual existence. Think of the

9

angels as guides to help you to remember to fulfill this plan and do it in an easy way. Angels can and will take the burden if you let them. Also, using optimum language when communicating with angels is important but not necessary. We will show you these words and phrases which will facilitate your communication with the angels and your spirit guides.

Many of you realize a change is in order and needed and desired, but are overwhelmed by the thought that it is arduous, difficult and almost impossible. You might also think that it requires reviewing some of your past thoughts and deeds of which you are not proud or which may be very painful to review. This is not necessary. God loves you unconditionally and there is nothing you could ever think or do to change that.

Removing the Fears

The releasing of fears begins with a quiet meditation. Be sure that you are alone and that you will be undisturbed. Ask God and the angels to assist you. You must have intent in your heart when you ask for something from the angels. By saying, "It is my intention and desire to release my fears to receiving love and a loving relationship," you let the angels know this is a powerful and sincere request. The angels will always grant what is in your heart. You may also ask the angels to release any blocks you may have to receiving love. Now that you have asked, release the job to the angels. You do not need to tell them how. You do not need to tell them when or where.

For example, if you desire and intend to have a loving relationship with a man, you might be tempted to say any of the following: "Please have that man, Bob, in accounting call me for a date this weekend." "Please have the phone ring this afternoon." Or, "Please let me run into him in the break room at work," etc. Perhaps Bob in accounting isn't really the man for you. The angels know more than you do at a superficial level of thinking. They will honor your request perhaps, but what you really are wanting is a relationship with more depth. Allow the angels time and freedom to honor your true intent and desire. Once you are in the habit of making requests to your angels and seeing them granted, you will enjoy shedding the problem from your hands into theirs. You can make a request, forget about it and relax. It will happen. We will talk about manifesting your intents and desires in this chapter. Also, you are not doing anything bad by giving your problems away to the angels. Your higher self will communicate and make you available when the cues or suggestions come that put you on the path to fulfilling your request. Remember, you do have free will and you do not have to follow the angels' guidance and suggestions.

The early morning hours are a pure and ripe time for meditation and squaring away one's thinking and plans for the day. In the early morning, there is time and there is peace. Start the day with a chakra clearing exercise or meditation, however brief. Start from the love and let the love be the motivation for your thoughts and actions during the day. Evening can be a busy time for the humans on your planet and is best ended by an evening meditation—even ten minutes of quiet solitary time to return to your essence. Starting and ending each day with acknowledgement and feeling the essence is a dramatic way to change the days and the nights. Also, at night the request to your angels to work with you in your dreams while you sleep is productive, too. You can ask the angels to work during the night to release blocks and fears that are motivating your thinking and actions. Seeing the whole picture is essential. You started as essence and are essence. Bare the essence. Remove the covering shell. The nightly observations you make are critical and progress you. Do not feel down or frustrated. This will meet fruition. Each day you can change by having the intent and desire to come from love rather than fear and hate.

The thoughts you have come out and have a lasting, permanent effect on the universe. Soon after, encase them in a bubble and give them to an angel to take to God for purification and to be returned to you as pure love. Do not allow these thoughts to stay free floating. Think about and notice, without judging, the comments and words of yourself and others.

Are the words showing love, caring and kindness, or not? If they are, then you know that they are coming from a love basis. If not, they are coming from another's fears and anger. This is the shell of the person controlling the words and actions rather than the higher self which will always come from love. The ego part of you does not love. It drives fear, anger and even hate into your lives, your words and your actions. When you realize it would be wonderful to relieve yourselves from the small stresses of every-day life this way, having a relaxed day rather than an anxiety-filled day makes all of the difference in the world. When you realize that you have thoughts or actions or words that are not coming from love, stop immediately and take a moment to ask the angels to take those thoughts and those actions to God for transmutation and they will turn into love and will come back to you and the person involved.

Let's say that you are having a disagreement with your partner. The goal is to love your partner unconditionally. Listen to your words. Are they coming from love? They may be coming from a fear basis. Fear that you aren't important. Perhaps fear that you don't count. And the old fear that you are not loved and appreciated. When you have a disagreement with someone, you should be addressing your words to the other's higher self, not the ego or the shell of the person. Sometimes you are hanging on to old anger for past deeds the other committed and that's what your argument is really about. Two people who are arguing from a fear basis will never resolve anything. Ask the angels to come into your conversation and keep you love based. The Archangel Gabriel is the angel of communication and she will help both people stay love-centered and will purify your words. Remember, you both must ask Gabriel to help. She cannot help without your permission. You do not need to speak aloud to ask.

When you are in a disagreement and you are coming from a love basis, you will find that issues that seemed so important lose their significance and fall away from you like water off of a hillside. The betterment of the other person becomes your unselfish goal. Problems are easily resolved. After all, even though you think superficially that it is the behavior of the other person you want to change, it is really the thinking they have before the behavior that needs to be elevated to a higher level. The new behavior will automatically follow.

Having the desire in your heart when you ask for angel assistance is all that matters. Do not worry if the words do not come out as you would like. The angels know your desire and intent when you hold it in your heart. You ask and yet you may feel fear for the perfect solution to come. You fear it may require work or change or expending energy that you do not have. Rest assured that with angel assistance we stress the ease of implementing the solutions.

Easy is the key word. We stand by daily and watch as you struggle with seeming problems and confrontations. We are here to ease your life. Take a moment to take a deep, cleansing breath and then recognize and see what is in your heart. Your true wishes and desires will show themselves now. You will feel joy, but you may also feel disbelief that so seemingly difficult a problem or situation could actually have a perfect and easy solution. Yet it is so. The more you request our assistance the more you will see and soon you will believe the truth. You did not come here to be alone and independent. Remember this truth. You are one with God and one with all other life. You are an integral part. Feel the joy as you melt into place in the story of God and man.

Above all else hold the desire for love in your heart. Hold the desire that all solutions come from love. This is being unselfish. There is no need for you to wish for specific solutions that benefit only you. Realize that having the desire and intent in your heart will make solutions come that are perfect for all and perfect in all directions of time. Do not tie our hands as we assist you. You can and will remember that there is a universal plan and you will release your desires to the universal mind and all-knowing God.

Thanking us for our help is gentle music to our ears. We are with you and we wish to serve you always. We rejoice and delight in your thoughts and words beckoning us to come and to assist you. We would like you to have daily habits of seeking and securing our help. Many deeds and tasks you do daily and on a regular basis can be speedily accomplished with our help. We wish to assist you as you drive your cars. We wish to assist you throughout your workday. We can help your telephone calls and other communications to go speedily and perfectly on their way. Archangel Gabriel wishes to assist you with all of your communications to bring the perfect and desirable results to you.

Archangel Raphael will always be present to guarantee your perfect health, vitality and energy to successfully go through your day. We are all here. We stand by. Call upon us more. Call upon us frequently and we have told you this does not make you dependent. It enlists us as well as your higher self for a more satisfying result in all of your endeavors. We give you gentle reminders of our presence and wishes to serve. You may see a bird fly across your path or a feather on the ground. We also whisper in your ear ideas and solutions or choices for you to consider. You may look at the clock or other item with the numbers "444" showing. These three-fours remind you that the angels are with you. Your daily work can be seemingly arduous, long or difficult, and yet we are here to erase those words so that you are effective, satisfied and the job is completed in the most perfect way. We love you unconditionally. You are perfect, whole and complete. Please include us. We wait for you. We sometimes get impatient and urge you and nudge you. We are so excited to be on your team!

Chapter 3

Love

The Magic of Love

Now we speak to you of good deeds. Deeds for those near and dear, for starting the love at home and in one's inner circle is how the ripple spreads across the water upon the pond. You have the eyes. You know the love and twinkle in your eyes that connect with your smile. Wear it always. Think about it and it will become more automatic. As you think and plan the good deed or as it spontaneously occurs from your heart, feel the warmth inside and feel that you are one with the recipient. Look into her eyes and you will see the magic occur. It is a magical connection with two people who, for at least a moment in time, feel as one. The eyes and the smile say, "I love you. I love you no matter what. Although we may withdraw from one another immediately, I have had the magic of oneness with you now." This magic will be here and there every day. Then it will occur more frequently. Your smile will come more often. You will do it on purpose more often. You will feel good, but you will see the joy that the other feels and you will hunger and thirst for that sight again and again in your day, in your life.

This grows the heart chakra very big. Your aura expands and touches everyone around you and they soak up your warmth like you drink in the moonlight into your soul. Then share your secret. You are a beacon and we will tell you this many times. Others come to you and will mimic you. Now, you will recognize this action in others' behaviors. Yes, you have seen it before countless times around you. Relax and experience the feeling right now. Stop reading for a moment and feel this beautiful warmth. It is the essence expanded large and all filling. There is no space or recess in which the essence is not. Look for the magic. You shall bring in the magic and herald the entire new year and millennium with this action. This can replace the stress. This is contagious. Let it grow. Watch it grow. You cannot stop it.

The trick of the mind occurs when two people come together and are artificial. The ego mind expects love and acceptance. The higher self knows love and knows love is there. The trick occurs when the mind feels it must look outward for this love. The love is there always. Look within to see it and recognize it.

The trick also occurs when the mind looks outward trying to create love artificially. "Should love, will love, can love" are all phrases the mind says to itself. The trick is in knowing that love is already existing. Too much time is taken up with these statements and stresses. Feel the love that is already there. The problem is not in making the love happen. The truth is in accepting the love that already exists. Yes, you can love each and everyone whom you see, hear and come in contact with whether in person or in the mind. You can because it is already so. Accept this and feel the warmth again. The pressure is off, right? It is easy to accept. Realize it. Just say to yourself, "Oh, I already do love you" (him, her, it or whatever). "This is easy. I can spread it." The point is that the mind thinks it cannot love or does not love and must trick itself into thinking it loves. Silly mind!

Opening to the flow and the rhythm and the current of life is only to release the hold and grasp you have on the present moment. Even though sometimes the present moment is about something tomorrow or next week or next year, allow the current to carry you along. No, this is not an aimless and irresponsible way to live. You will make the decisions that are right for you because you will know the right answer when it comes along. Feeling the path to take. Feeling the answer to make. Seeing your way clearly. Trusting in yourself. "I can make my life be the way that I want it." More of the affirmations will come. For now, relax and enjoy the flow. The answer cannot come if you are still grasping the problem today.

The affirmation is only to remind you of the realness of the request and the realness of the solution. When it is asked from the heart it will be done. Reinforce with affirmations to tell the ego it is not appealing. Hold nothing back and release all. Only in releasing and letting go will you feel the power that you have, the power that you are. Try it, you'll like it!

Driving desire and driving ambition keeps you focused. But on what? That which you think is real but is not. That which you think is important but is not. That which appears so glorious but is not. That which brings happiness but does not. Happiness is within you now. The answer is always to go within. Focusing on the happiness inside of you can allow it to come out and engulf you. You will radiate happiness and others will want also to manifest this feeling. Happiness is the feeling, the true feeling of love, of experiencing love and giving love. This is the bliss you seek. The time is now.

Words for Him

The gentle and beautiful truth resides inside you. This is your tender, loving side. This is the real you. As gentle words fall from your lips to another's ear, know that they take love with them and that love is received by your listeners. It heals and it soothes. Love says, "I am just like you inside. We are all one." Our gentle words tell another that you not only love, but also care and appreciate their deeds, actions and their very being. Let these gentle words fall from your lips often. This is not a feminine exercise. This is a refreshing exercise of the love within you, your very essence, which is like all others around you. To communicate your truth and express your love is a powerful way to live. You have overcome fears and ego's obstacles to rise above and follow your mission. Your service to all humanity and Mother Earth begins with this simple expression of appreciation and respect. Your love is given freely and unconditionally to all at all times. Yes, this is a powerful yet gentle and fulfilling way to live. As others see your example, whether they are male or female, they will see and yearn to know your secret. Share it with them. Let them know they can release their fears to God and the angels and be in the magical, wondrous world of love and peace.

Romantic Love

The pure and simple romantic love of two people for one another is a beautiful occurrence. Liken it to the growing of the elm and becoming stronger by the day, branching out and creating itself anew. The bond between two will bind and entwine them for eons and throughout eternity. The love is deep and magical for it creates a new life. A new life for both as they grow together and nourish and support one another.

The news one receives affects the two. All actions, deeds and thoughts affect the united souls. To have a seeming pain can be relieved by the love embodied in the partner. All creation is seen as a magical event on this adventure of the two. To come together and share a life with this bond is part of your purpose on this Earth. No one shall walk alone. Yet, we see you struggle as you search to identify the soul which waits for you. You will recognize the other half of your pair as your very essence suddenly shines brighter and bolder until you think it cannot increase any more. You will be ready to forfeit all to be one with this person, but you shall not forfeit. You both only shall gain. You shall be steadfast and true as the other seeks to lean on you and to feel your strength in all of her days.

Giving and loving is easy. You think of only the other as you go through your day. Nothing else is important because it cannot compete with the feeling of love and yearning that you now experience. And yet, as ego comes along and shows that it will settle in and make a threesome, instead we watch you struggle to regain the feelings of the first love moment that you shared. Set ego aside. There is not room for him in this relationship. Recognize when ego is speaking through your partner's mouth with his very words. Know that these sad thoughts and words are not for you and that they are not intended for you by your true love. Relax and do not fear his love for you has died or gone away. Know this truth: love is stronger than all. Ego can only hide the source of love but never affect it. Reach out your hand to show that your love is still there burning stronger than ever as you make your journey together. You have planned this. You will survive this and you shall always be at home in the arms of the other for you are one. Safeguard this love as it is dear. Do not let any threat to this love come your way and find a place in your heart. You will grow in love together for that is meant to be.

Receiving the Love

Welcome to the universe. A place and an existence of love. We wish you to open your hearts even more than they are to receive the tremendous love that comes to you constantly from so many places, levels and dimensions. This is love you deserve. This is love with your name on it. This is love that has bounced back to you from your kind deeds to another. Love is the truth. Love is. We wish to help you understand that you are a being of love and that you are surrounded by love constantly. The love flows through you continuously as you live your life every minute of every day. Love is what makes the engine go. Ego is what tries to slow it down.

In the beginning there was only God and God is love. You were born from a thought of God and are completely infused with His love. This is part of your makeup. This is the basis and foundation of your makeup. This cannot change nor would God ever want it to change. You are tied to Him. You are part of Him and He is part of you. There is nowhere you walk without the power of his presence with you. There is no breath that you take that you do not inspire Him. There is no hand that reaches to help you that is not Him. There is no tear you can cry that cannot be turned into love by Him. There is no feeling in your soul that cannot be shared, transmuted and changed into love and come back to you as warmth and love from Him. Know these truths. They shall comfort you all of your days on the Earth and when you or your loved ones cross over. Do not forget this very important, exciting, powerful truth. You are not a separate being. You are never alone. We have told you this and remind you of this in case you have felt this is too good to be true.

You can in your mind's eye see every man, woman and child on Earth holding hands. Visualize this now. You are all in a giant circle around the Earth. You are linked and connected. Your souls are joined and cannot ever be divided. Realize that joined as one around the planet you are all facing inward, focusing on and embracing your host, Mother Earth. She needs this bond strengthened. Recognize this and teach this to others. The warm caress of humanity united will heal man, the Earth, and all therein. Visualize this every day. See the sleeping ones awaken to these truths and the caress becomes more loving and kind. You are here for this reason. You are an important part of the whole. The whole united is a dynamic, strong and powerful presence that knows only love. This we share with you. There is an urgent need to activate this cycle. The angels stand ready to assist you. They, too, are a part of the whole.

The winding road leads the tale of the never-ending story of love. The continuous flow and recycling of the love within. It spreads to all and never ends. It weaves a spell of protection, life and happiness. It is contagious and ever moving. You are a link in the chain. The spell must be cast over the millions. Feel the love within grow brighter. Feel the essence enlarge you and surround you. It reaches out fingers of love to connect with another and reminds you that all are one. All are one with God. This is in your memory. Cherish these thoughts. There are no separate beings. All are one. The ribbon of love reaches outs and entwines all. This is needed to heal the Earth. This ribbon goes around the world, one by one, day by night it travels to remind all that you are connected to each other. Be kind to yourself as this affects all of the others.

We are here to help you remember and visually join hands together to hold the thought and feeling of love in unison. As you see and feel the black clouds of anger, hate and fear in the Earth, in your country, in your neighborhood and in your immediate surroundings, hold that thought. Ask the angels and God to transmute that thought of fear into thoughts and feelings of love. Visualize and see the black clouds disappear and become the beautiful white light which is God and love. See this white light spread and encompass all. It grows bigger and brighter. It is spreading rapidly and cannot be stopped. Ego has no power or existence here. All is love. Only love. Practice this visualization every day. This is important. The time has come for you to act. Remember and take part in the plan which you volunteered to do. You will feel the love within grow stronger and more beautiful each and every time you practice this exercise. God bless you. You are a miracle worker.

Chapter 4

Spirituality

Spirituality is a continuing and continuous process. It is an existence. You cannot deny this aspect of your being. It has been with you since your first creation by God. Many do and will continue to try to hide from this aspect. It is more than an aspect. It is. This is not religion for one can change religions every day. Religion hopes for and inspires spirituality. Yet many do not have both. Spirituality exists where religion may not. Spirituality is one with the essence which is you. Your spirituality can be hidden for a whole lifetime only to be revealed when you pass over at the end of the physical life. The spiritual self is the higher self. Spirituality teaches you how to treat yourself and others. It is in conflict with the ways that ego tells you to treat yourself and others.

Spirituality knows its ways are correct and divine. Ego tries and tries with strong words and deeds and actions to convince your higher self that it is right. Ego is a reactive entity. Spirituality just is. Spirituality is for everyone. We are all the same. Spirituality tells us we are all the same. That we are one with each other. Ego preaches that we are better than others. Ego will also tell us we are no good. What ego says changes constantly. It is ego that is responsible for moods that change all of the time and frequently throughout your day.

Being centered in spirituality makes the entire day good regardless of anything that can occur. Ego has you up and down all day and half the night telling you one thing and then another. Have you ever counted how many times your mood changed in a day? What about how many times your emotions changed from good to bad to worse and around again? This is ego. Ego controls. Ego is lost if it cannot control your thoughts, deeds and actions. Ego is a dictator. All actions from ego are designed to keep ego and the basis of fear alive. When you feel afraid know that ego is controlling your life at that moment.

Tell the angels with intent and desire in your heart that you are willing to release this fear and that you are asking for their help for you to do so. They are immediately on the scene. If the fear does not leave, ask the angels to tell you what lesson you are wanting to learn now so that the situation will change and the fear will be released. Recognizing when ego is in the driver's seat is important. Know him well for he knows you well and drives you and pushes all of your buttons. If there was a person who controlled your life and dictated your thoughts, actions and deeds constantly 24-hours a day and told you to become angry, hurt, jealous, feel unworthy, feel antagonistic, and other negative behavior, you would surely stop associating with that person.

Spirituality exists in everyone continuously. Ego is a rival and would like to replace and omit spirituality. Holding love in your heart is being spiritually alive. Sending that same love out to your brothers and sisters is spirituality. Holding the safety and well being of Mother Earth in your heart is spirituality. Recognize all that spirituality encompasses. There are not degrees. It just is. It exists and can only be hidden by that outer shell or take back seat to hate, anger, and hostility. We, the angels, archangels, ascended masters and God, exist in this spirituality with you. We are all one. We are one on a journey together. Be encouraged. You do well. You will get better. You will rejoice in the splendor of loving with God and living a spiritually evolved life.

Chapter 5

Ego

There is a controller in the thick fabric shell that has accumulated attempting to hide the burning essence of love within. He is ego. The ego seems very powerful and in control often. He is not, however, as strong as the powerful essence which is you. He is only an interloper who skillfully attempts to keep your mind busy with his wishes and demands. You have only to recognize he is the source of your dissatisfaction and you will be on the way to eliminating and quieting him. Notice the remarks seem obsessive, cruel, and unfriendly. When you have these feelings about yourself or your fellow man, know that ego is running the show. Ask the angels to assist you in transmuting these current thoughts and to help to remove ego from control.

Knowing that ego is active is the first step. You need to tell the angels that you are willing to release blocks or fears connected with the main subject of what you are thinking about. Sometimes we see you planning your words to be ready for an encounter with another. These are unfriendly and unloving words which seek to insult and overpower another. You know these thoughts do not come from love. See that they really are an attack on another. Anytime you have a conversation which does not come from love, realize that it is an attack on or against your brothers and sisters. We have shown you, dear one, what to do with these negative thoughts. Do not judge yourself for having them. Very often asking the angels to assist you, taking a deep, cleansing breath, and having the intent and desire in your heart to eliminate this kind of thinking is all that is necessary to conquer the seeming problem.

Asking for angels, a cleansing breath, and intent and desire are very powerful. More powerful than ego. Ego is, however, persistent and you may need to repeat the process to oust him more than once a day. Taking time to get centered in love can melt away and eliminate ego's control in that present moment. Soon this technique becomes habit and you can do it easily and frequently. The strength and power you have can accomplish anything you truly desire. Call on the angels as they are very, very strong and powerful. They stand ready to assist you. All they ask is that you thank them for their help.

So, this is who ego is and what he does. Fire him. You do not need or want this monster in your life. You can allow or not allow ego to exist. It can be very exciting to make the discovery that ego is in charge when you are feeling bad and to know that you can change it immediately. You can will the ego and his control away. The angels will help you. Please ask them to do so.

Separateness

The desire and instant thought and yearning you have to be unique and separate from all others is a stumbling block in your life. All man is one with God and one with each other. The essence of pure love seeks to remind you of that and will keep all together. Because you have free will, you can allow ego to run rampant and strive to keep you different and separate. You may believe this illusion. You may and will judge others daily and seek to maintain your individual identity by maintaining separateness from others. This goes against your very essence and purpose. Realize this now. There is oneness with all. This is the way it has been created and it cannot change. This is God's will. This is also the will of your essence.

It must be your goal to remember this, practice and live this truth. You can do it. Take off that outer coat or shell that keeps you tied up in thoughts of separateness. The personality which is you will not basically change. It will modify as you learn your lessons and advance spiritually.

This is your plan. This is your true desire. This is the purpose of your life here. While serving yourself and growing spiritually, you will be fortified by the giving and serving of others which is the true purpose of all. You may be a teacher, a healer, a friendly face and voice at a needed time. You may be a nurturer or a tender of animals in God's kingdom. It is all the same. Each part of the one serves the other. There is plenty to do striving to perfection and the perfect existence from which we have wavered. All will return and must return now in this new millennium.

We will each do our part and all will flow smoothly as long as we recognize and accept the true desire in our heart. Your angels stand by to wait for this moment of truth. You must feel it and acknowledge it often as it is the lifeline to your survival and to the survival of all.

The occupation of your mind is easily taken over by ego. Ego will occupy your mind with worrying, conversations to yourself and others, nonsense vengeful thoughts, etc. You know how it goes. We will assist you with wiping the slate of your mind clean by saying aloud or silently, "Do not tolerate these negative, useless thoughts. This is a time for me to quiet my mind and listen for the thoughts from my higher self, God, and ascended masters and the angelic realm."

Picture in your mind's eye or see with your third eye (the eye of psychic vision) a group of angels around you. You may say, "There are five angels around me now," or you may ask for more. Now say, "I am listening to the angels and receiving the message or messages they want to communicate to me." If there is a seeming problem that has been occupying your mind frequently, ask the angels to give you some insight as to why you may be facing this challenge and what growth lesson you could have instead. Be patient. The angels will respond to your requests. Should ego jump back in, repeat that you will not tolerate ego's control of your mind now.

When dealt with powerfully and firmly, ego will abandon temporarily. When you notice ego has returned, you know what to do. The more you use time for communicating with angels the more easily you will get rid of ego. You may also ask the angels to release the hold that ego seems to have on you at this time. Please do not judge yourself if ego returns again and again. Practicing getting rid of ego is good for your spiritual growth. Taking control of your mind is not a waste of time.

Acceptance

Acceptance and unconditional love are partners. Flowing with the energy allows one to accept another person just as they are and just as they have been created, perfect, whole and complete. The outer shell that they wear means nothing. There is no thought of trying to change the other person because you know that he has come to take on his challenges and grow just as you are doing. This is unconditional love. The loving acceptance you have for your family, friends and associates comes from the basis of unconditional love. This love embraces all and says to others, "I love and accept you just the way you are." This love reaches out to the higher self of all others. This does not mean that others may treat you badly and it is okay with you. You shall move away from those who do. As you decide to move away from those relationships, there will be no judging or condemning. Distance yourself as you will, but send them love and light. There is no wish on your part to have others do things your way. Everyone is different and you allow them to be so. You revel in and enjoy the uniqueness of others' personalities. You know that even with the differences among you, you are all the same, all are one. Trusting others and accepting others is no threat to you. Ego is not involved. You keep him away. You extend your love and kindness to all.

The Miracle of the Seven

We will now give to you the seven signs. These signs are clues to keep you focused and on track. These seven signs are magical. Love is the only thing that is real. All else is magic and illusion. The first sign is hostility.

You must recognize the feeling of hostility. You will hear it in your tone of voice. You will feel the heat in your body rise. You will feel the energy that drives this feeling. This feeling is based in fear. It gets its energy from fear and its direction and motivation from ego. The second sign is evil thoughts. The mind tricks you into thinking and planning to do evil acts. This feeling also comes from fear. It, too, is driven by ego. The third sign is jealousy. This is a feeling of emptiness and a feeling of no power. Fear creates this feeling. The fourth sign is negativity. This feeling of frustration comes from fear. The fifth sign is envy. This feeling of others having more is caused by fear. The sixth sign is vengeance. Ego and fear unite to create and drive this feeling of evening up the score. The seventh sign is hate. Fear and desperation give rise to this unhappy feeling.

Do you see, dear one, that we use these strong words? It is necessary that we do so. This is an important concept. This you can and will conquer. All of these signs rise and are born from fear. What is this great fear that creates these destructive feelings which bear the fruit of unhappiness and separateness from your brothers and sisters? Only love is real. Fearing that you are not loved by God can become an overwhelming experience. Ego is only too happy to jump on this train of destruction and drive it on. Study these words. It is imperative that you recognize these feelings as signs. The presence of any one or more of these signs must be realized and acknowledged immediately. When these signs are present, it means that you have moved away from God as part of your illusion. The only way to end these feelings is to remind yourself that you are loved by God. This is the truth and you remember it well.

Dear one, we have spoken that you are godly and loved by God. Every part of you is God. You cannot escape this even though at times you feel forlorn, forgotten and try to do so. He is everywhere. These rough words are to teach you the magic. The magic is that even though you may have any one of these signs which is the worst thing in the world to feel, think that you can change it in an instant. Change it immediately by remembering the love you receive. You are love. Stop at this moment and feel and see your essence expand. Ask the essence to expand and burn brighter as you receive more and more love from God in this present moment. The essence expands and is all-powerful. This power is yours. The love is yours to use. This love is stronger and the only truth when compared to any of the seven signs. Do see this, beloved one. Know that there is a power stronger than any hate or evil you may seem to face.

There is no room in your heart for these dark spots. We stand here to tell you this and to help you at what may seem a dark hour when these signs seem to overwhelm you. God is here. We, the ascended masters, and we, the archangels and Earth angels and your spirit guides, are here. All around you are your brothers and sisters. They are here to help you, too. Feel the cataclysmic power you hold in your hand and in your heart. These signs are conquered. They trigger the chain reaction of the magic that occurs. They trigger the thought process which brings you back to love and back to God.

Recognize that these signs hold no power over you. They have no power at all. Ego would like to run this show and drive these feelings but you know that even without us you have the power to vanquish all. You are strong. You are perfect, whole and complete. Only love is real. Only God is. This lesson you are learning and you will see that any other negative emotion or feeling you may seem to be preoccupied with pales in comparison to the power of love. God is with you as you share this important lesson with others. You will heal the world one person at a time. One lesson at a time. One act of kindness and love at a time. You are now full of tremendous healing energy. Heal yourself, your neighbor and send the healing love and kindness around the world. God is with you now.

Chapter 6

Fear and Anger

The words we use will stand on their own and among their own. Each thought is surrounded by a cloud of essence which makes any thought larger. A thought has energy of its own. People speak their minds clearly and freely on your sphere. The goal and purpose is to defeat ego status and purifying the thoughts is then a simple exercise or expression of love. As you know, if it does not come from love it comes from fear via the hate. So many of you feel anxious much of the time because the ego is being fed instead of being put aside so the nurturing of the soul will occur unimpeded. The soul nourishes itself by its very existence. It is only love. Many people on your sphere feel anxiety because the hateful words come out when they know in their hearts and souls that these words, deeds and thoughts are at odds with their very being and intention.

Recall the joy of uttering loving words. Recall the severity of the angry words and the physical, emotional, and psychic feeling of them. Think of these negative words as negative ions attached to and radiating from your body and that they attract more negative energy. Like to like. A daily or hourly immersion in the positive ions of love will neutralize, cleanse and eliminate the negative ions and negative energy. This is done through soulful meditation, affirmations, prayer and making the essence fill the physical body and the auric field. This is the starting point. The basis of all building blocks we will add. Let spirit lead the way. This is the goal, this setting aside of the ego. Always speaking your truth can become a habit difficult to break.

Talking is the subject for now. The talking must elicit the truth. For one's words are dear and must be dear. The light must shine each and every time the voice is heard. Taking back the words cannot happen and is complicated to try. Each word is a thought personified and given life. Each phrase uttered or thought takes action and has effect. The distant realms will hear these words and thoughts. Refrains of music are also heard near and far. These times hold much anger and fear. The residue is like black soot that blankets the land, the soul and the heart. Teaching purification of thought and deed is your burden and load. These deeds are more important than ever now.

Each word and thought is a gift to someone or to all. Is it a gift you want opened? Or should the recipient hide this gift forever? It is your choice when you speak, not theirs. Thoughts become actions and actions become events. The events are a ripple in a big, big pond. When you think that your words become events and last for an eternity, are you sure you want to speak other than speaking your truth? To wound is to maim and maiming is forever. The individual waits for your words. The world waits for your words. Make them special. The words of love can flow through you in a liquid speech that is beautiful to the ear. Joyous notes make the souls of the listeners sing. The listeners then become the speakers and their words may fall beautifully on another's ear as did yours.

Each morning start the day with the light and airy feeling of joyous love that is bursting your soul and bursting out of you to be spread upon the forms of life you are in contact with every day. Redeeming the unwanted words is more difficult. It takes time and does not easily erase. The eraser is not big enough.

The kind deeds you do also ripple the pond water. A generosity from the heart can be a mere "hello" to a stranger on the street. It can be a smile to a forlorn soul struggling through the day without your insight and without remembering that she is loved completely. Your smile will tell her that. The deeds of kindness and gentleness to our animals who are angels sent to us by God are precious. Our pets look at us with adoring, unconditional love and shall remind us over and over that we were created perfect to be adored, loved and held in high esteem by all. The actions mean initiative is being taken to change the world one small piece at a time. Mountains can easily be moved by intention and desire.

More time for respite is good for the body and the soul. Tire not, for all is easy with our help. We have promised you that the path of love is easy and simple. This is not hard work. By remembering the love you have for each and every being is the first part. Acknowledge these feelings. Let them grow. Feed them and water them with the pure love of God which rains down on every one of you. Ignore the fabric shell and let the rain of his love dissolve it away. It will happen before your eyes and you will see the change. It is not a change in them but a change you have experienced and initiated. Their part is to respond to your gesture and respond they will, dear one. You will feel the return of their love a thousand fold when you look into their eyes which are the windows of their soul and of yours as well. Yes, when you see another, it is also a gaze into your true self. Honor the other and hold him in high esteem. There is only more love to gain.

Let us talk about the fear and the anger. Fear and anger are from the ego and drive many a thought and deed on your planet. The fear wraps around the soul and the light of the essence may burn dim. However, a breath of air from pure love ignites that flame. As you see another reacting or acting from fear you can send them more love. This is when they need it most. This is when you must give. Remember your mission. Whatever it is, it is in addition to service to others. Recognize and realize that you may only need to send a smile to a person to bail her out of the depths of despair in her day. Rejoice that so much can be done so easily.

Releasing the Fear

Releasing the fears related to giving and receiving love involve a simple exercise. With intent and desire in your heart call for your angels. Tell them, "I am willing to release the fears regarding giving and receiving love." The fears sometime have a strangling hold on us and we may need to do this exercise several times. Remember, the angels can miraculously and immediately work or act to fulfill your request. You will notice that you feel differently after this exercise. When you are sending love to others you are sending it to the higher self.

Your love message does affect that tough outer shell created by ego. It tells the other person that you love them unconditionally regardless of any flaws or shortcomings they think that they seem to have. There are many words to say "I love" and there are also many actions. As you give love to others, you will immediately see that you are receiving love from them at the same time. It may only be a brief acknowledgment of the love you share. The other person's ego is going to jump into the situation quite fast. Ego does not like these exchanges that occur with the higher self. The other person's ego may strike out with words to insult you or to hurt you. These words or actions are designed by ego to alienate you from others.

Ego wants a separateness. He does not like the truth that you are one with all creation. You may seem to think that sending out the love message is risky. We guarantee you that love will be reciprocated. Do not worry if you do not recognize the love message from the other. Practice this every single day and soon you will begin to notice all of the signs of love coming from others. Oftentimes love sends a message that words are not necessary at this time. Keep sending the love and you will overcome these fears that you must release to the angels. This is our favorite job, to assist in filling you and others with 100% love.

Chapter 7

Problem Solving

Preparing for the angels' visit is a simple and yet more complex process. Yes, merely wanting to speak to angels or asking in your heart or aloud one can do easily. The hard part is remembering to do so. Why are you so reluctant to ask for help which will always be given? Ask and release the problem to us. To hear angels speaking or communicating in other ways is easy, yet requires some cleansing preparation to make you a stronger receiver of information.

Please relax and open your heart to our answers. The genuine feeling of being uplifted shows that you have given the problem to us and that we have received the problem from you. Yes, give it up completely to us. Understand, dear little one, that the solution will come from God, from love which is all. You may not recognize the solution has arrived at first, but trust that it indeed has. It may wear another face and look differently from what you might have in mind.

Let us show you examples in which we await your requests and hope you will enlist us:

> * Waiting for a bus and wanting a short wait
> * Looking for a taxicab
> * Preparing an easy, nutritious meal
> * Calming a fussy child
> * Helping a bored child
> * Wanting a new dress
> * Doing household chores
> * Needing more money
> * Getting to work on time
> * Getting a promotion, changing into the perfect job for you

* Qualifying to buy that dream home
* Wanting a safe road trip or a safe drive to work
* Finding an address on a strange street
* Getting the car repaired quickly and inexpensively
* Having the right person answer your ad for a job that you have open
* The gas gauge shows empty and you want to make it to the gas station
* Staying healthy during outbreaks of cold and flu
* You want to lose the craving for all of those desserts.

The problems can be great or small. We stand ready. The process of giving and releasing your problem to us involves three steps: giving, releasing and recognizing. It isn't even always necessary that you do recognize the solution when it comes, for the solution will come and it will come from love and be perfect for you at that time. The important thing is the feeling you have to release it and that the solution is en route. Feel lighter, happier, calmer, and not obsessed with the problem any longer. The problem can overwhelm you and take over your life, every waking moment and take your sleep time away, too. Feel as free and happy as you do when you hand your keys over to the attendant at the car wash. You release the problem of the dirty car to someone who will eliminate the problem easily.

If you sit and brainstorm and try every possible solution you and a hundred other people can think of, you still may not find the solution that is perfect for you and any others involved at that time. God and the angels will always give you the perfect solution.

What if the solution isn't to your liking and isn't the solution you asked for? There are times when the only thing you can see is the problem and a certain solution. God and the angels always see the big picture. We see past, present and future. We know what special challenges you have asked for in this life. We know that you want to grow with defeating problems. You want to learn the lesson the first time. We know that you don't want to face the same problem time and again and never accomplish what you came to do in this life. When you trust God and the angels, you are trusting your higher self which also knows all of this information. You are very wise. You can call a friend for answers or you can trust your own wise self.

The work of the day begins with plans. Plan for a smooth-running day. Make plans with your higher self to circumvent any unnecessary problems. Yes, some problems are necessary because they herald the challenges you planned to face and conquer in this lifetime. What we want to do is to help you to see the ways of preventing unnecessary problems, not the problems that are needed to teach you small lessons. They stimulate growth and learning in your life.

As you grow and learn so can you teach others these same things. Positive thinking is a necessary skill to attune. Speaking negatively as if you already have a given problem will surely bring that same dreaded situation into your life. Phrases such as, "I don't have enough money;" "I am getting sick again;" "I'm sure the mail will be full of bills I can't pay," must be omitted from usage. Instead, manifest that all will be well. "I have enough money to meet all of my obligations and needs." "I seem to have a physical problem here. What is the lesson I need to learn? I will learn it now and not have the experience of being sick to learn this lesson."

Invite the angels into your life to hand problems over to them. They will take these problems and give them to God for a divine and perfect solution. Other problems are simple and you are completely qualified and experienced to find the perfect solutions yourself. Speaking of your seeming problems to others only reinforces their existence and makes them part of your reality. Instead, think of the solution and dwell on the wonderful results that will come.

Choices

The choices that are made by you and others around you reflect the feelings of the ego or those feelings tied up in your fabric shell. Choices must be made from the heart which means the higher self is the source. Only the higher self, God and the angels can see the whole picture of action and consequences for all based on the choices made. When you exclude the higher self from the process undesirable consequences can occur. The higher self will do what is best, regardless of what the ego has to say about the action. Satisfying ego cannot be done by the higher self. The ego resists and fights and attempts to override. Remember, the voice of the higher self is a soft, gentle song while the sound from ego is harsh, loud and can be literally terrifying.

When you give the seeming problem to the angels and to God, it is a great occasion because you have started down the road to a divine and perfect solution. The ego would like the solution to happen immediately and dramatically and it's even better if it makes one feel bad about himself or another. Sometimes on your Earth it is easy to react immediately. The habit of pausing and reflecting and then speaking your truth is actually easier yet you may need divine help for you to make this a habit. Ego is as strong as you allow him to be. Do not turn the keys to happiness over to him.

Choices made must reflect an influence that goes along with your divine mission on this Earth in this life at this time. Or, you may be a link or an instrument of the mission of another person near you. Trust the choices made by the higher self. Trust, relax and know that you are safe with these answers. Pat yourself on the back for being brave, as change and new habits often scare one. Tell the angels you are willing to release the blocks to good communication and to making the right choices. They will help you but you must take the first step.

The first step in any change you are to do is to tell the angels you are willing to release the blocks. This gives the angels permission to come in and take them, purify them and return them to you in the form of simple, true, divine love. This is a good exercise to do before going to sleep. The angels stay up all night anyway. Give them something to do! Your requests to your angels are beautiful music to them and they rejoice in being of assistance to you whom they love so dearly and unconditionally. After you have slept and the busy angels have done their part, you will feel refreshed. Have you not awakened in the morning in the past and felt that some of your problems have melted away during the night as if by magic? This is the work of God's angels. This is their gift to you who are so holy and precious in their sight. Nothing will ever change that.

Easing Up on Your Treatment of Yourself

So many feel responsibility means taking the flack for all that occurs. This is not so. Cause and effect work differently as you will see. The rough and critical treatment of oneself is not necessary and is detrimental to the psyche. The spiritual self is perfect, whole and complete. Mistakes occur and need to be corrected. Do not allow ego to have you take blame and punishment ever. This life is about working out problems and challenges. Certainly not all decisions made are always perfect. You need assistance from the angelic realm. Again, we ask that you trust us and your higher self (which are one) to make these decisions. Do not dread them and emphasize them and allow them to become a big deal. The problems are needing choices to be made just as you walk through the produce department of the grocery store and choose which fruit to buy and which not to buy. One's imagination can grow any problem into a mountain that seemingly cannot be overcome. Make these seeming problems no larger than stones across a brook that you lightly and easily step on to cross the water. Be not surprised that life's matters can be reduced to small situations for you to easily conquer. You will get what you expect. Do not allow the problem to attach itself to you. Keep it at a distance.

All is well when we reach out to you. Help us make the connection complete. Your free will prevents many solutions from reaching you. Open the channels and let us in. We merely remind you that you have the power, strength and wisdom to solve your seeming problems. The higher self knows all and can see all. The higher self is in touch with the universal wisdom which is God. Each and every day walk with us and let us walk with you. Much of your Earth time is wasted on worrying, thinking and fretting. Control the mind. Evict the ego. All will be perfect.

Chapter 8

Reflection and Judgment

Reflection is an act from the basis of spirituality. Judgment is done entirely by ego. During reflection one remembers the day and notices those thoughts, deeds or actions that one would not repeat. There is no judgment involved, therefore, no punishment. A mistake is only a mistake at worst. It may not even be a mistake at all. During reflection one looks at the situation in a semi-analytical way. The cause and effect are noticed and found interesting. You may dissect it and discover the whys, etc., but that is not necessary.

Merely notice if ego was involved. The answer is usually yes. You may decide that ego will not have permission to choose those words, actions or deeds again. Reflection notices the growth lesson involved. Reflection asks the angels to help release fears and blocks or asks the angels to help you to choose the right words, the gentle words in the same situation. When your words punish another this is ego again. Ego in control. Ego is out asking another to judge you. If you are feeling that you are being unfairly judged by others, you can count on the fact that you have been judgmental, too. This is a way that we see in a mirror to know that what we are doing needs to be omitted from our behavior. Thank the person mentally or aloud for calling your attention to an area in your life that you can improve upon.

Now, do not judge yourself for having said or done the wrong thing. Merely correcting the behavior is all that God and the angels ask. It can be painful to reflect if ego is in charge. Evaluating your worth at the end of the day based on what was or was not said or what was or was not done is ego's way of putting you down and giving you a false set of values to live by. This is ego judging you. Know that every day no matter what you have said or done that it does not change your worth or value as a person. You are still the perfect, whole and complete person God made you and God still loves you exactly the same as He will tomorrow whether you correct your mistakes or not.

You are not changing your behavior to please God. You are changing your behavior to grow and advance spiritually. You want to improve. Feel the warmth, joy and bliss that radiate inside of you and surround you when you have truly grown from a situation or an action. Yes, God is proud of you. Be proud of yourself. Do not pat yourself on the back so hard that if you fail to correct another behavior, you judge yourself and feel unworthy. This is ego's trick. Do not put him in charge.

Evening is a time to reflect. A joyous occasion to celebrate the day's accomplishments and manifestations and interactions, the time to erase and intend to deny the ego the enjoyment of judgment. Judging others and yourself is unnecessary and unproductive. Remember, God is not a punishing God. So, there is no judgment and no judgment day. The reflection is necessary to evaluate and learn the lessons of the day that have come through and that you have attracted to you. Mistakes are made as a part of life, certainly, a part of life on the complex planet you live on. You are surrounded daily by others who may have negative influence on the ones surrounding them. Do not deny and try to escape these people. They have been attracted to you for one or more reasons so that each results in growth and more love between both of you.

Big lessons can come in small packages and incidents. During your times of reflection in the evening, without judging, notice and review your words, deeds and actions. If they did not come from love for others as well as for yourself, how would you change the same situation if repeated? And it will be repeated. Maybe with someone else or somewhere else, but the underlying purpose will be the same. Mistakes are only to be corrected. You will get another chance to do so. Mistakes are not to be punished. They are to be corrected. The angels will assist you with your intent and desire to them to help you. Tell them that you are willing to release the blocks to loving this other person and understanding her now. When you are willing to release the blocks and you ask the angels to help you, improvement will be made. Growth will occur. You will smile and feel and enjoy the satisfaction of improving yourself and taking another step along your path.

Aloneness

You yearn to have time to reflect, yet when alone you become lonely. Let us explain the value of time spent with oneself. It is to be appreciated. During these busy times one needs to create time for useful aloneness. This is time for meditation and reflection. A time for noticing without judging. Take this time to marvel at life in this universe. Marvel at the creations of God. All are perfect, whole and complete. You are the flower among these plants that grow reaching up for sunlight and nourishment. Your spiritual soul seeks this nurturing and yet can give nurturing back to you. This is cyclic. God has created all. Allow the beautiful appreciation to occur.

Anticipation

Anticipation is an exciting feeling for you. We, too, anticipate. We anticipate and know of good coming your way. We do not have a time element here so we do not watch the clock as you do with your excitement over possible events to come. Everything you do is exciting to us. We see you as perfect, whole and complete because you are. We see the goodness in you and in your deeds and actions when sometimes you are totally unaware that you have said or done something wonderful. You delight us constantly.

We wish for you to ignore and not to criticize yourself for certain deeds and actions that you commit from time to time. Mistakes occur and you know how we feel about that. For now, feel the excitement and delight you have as you anticipate right now an occurrence that you may have felt was very routine. For example, you are coming home at the end of your workday. Yes, your partner is there or your pet is there and, yes, you smile to see them. Think of this meeting a little differently. Think of this time as if it was a great and grand moment in your life—as if you had not seen this perfect person who loves you so much in a long, long time. You would be high on anticipation!

Think of the ordinary and common as a great and beautiful gift. This person loves you unconditionally and you feel the same way about her or him. Snatch these events and transform them into something beautiful because they really are. Bring excitement into your life this easily! Do it often. As you take the garbage out the back gate, get high on the excitement of seeing the neighbor's beautiful tree, the pathway to a neighbor's house, or anything you can look at anew. These are gifts you can give your soul any time. Do it often. Do it when you feel the least able to do so. This is when you need it most. Share this simple idea with everyone. It is exciting and contagious!

Chapter 9

Eliminating Pain

Now we speak of pain and the ordeal one goes through on your planet. You see pain is impossible with spirit. The pain is a trick of the mind by ego. It has directed and executed this order for you. You are not deserving of this and God never assigns you this situation to master for the sake of mastering a problem. There is no test from God that comes in the form of pain. Since the pain is an illusion manufactured by ego, it is also possible to eliminate it. Sometimes you may choose pain as a method to bring about a positive result. Often the mortals are weary of life and think they long for a physical rest. What one really is needing is a time of respite for the soul to renew and cleanse itself from the accumulation of daily debris and negative energies. Cleansing away these negative energies could be done daily for optimum spiritual and physical health.

Sometimes the mind will punish itself in anticipation of being punished by God or others. Yet you know there is no punishing God. Mistakes are to be corrected only. Eliminating pain in your life can start with a foundation of loving yourself unconditionally. You know that you love others this way and so must you love yourself this way, too. Do not allow the ego to tell you otherwise. You long to be perfect, yet we have told you that you are already perfect, whole and complete. When you seem to think that you have pain for any reason and from any cause, do not tolerate this illusion. Meditating and asking the higher self why you have chosen this will enlighten you. You may have to be persistent to get your answers as sometimes your receptivity is not optimal.

Your higher self may direct you to a healer of some kind, whether a licensed physician or another type of healer, but you still need to learn the lesson for which you have asked. You have asked for the experience and attracted it to you. Learn why by going within and questioning and getting your answer. A frequent habit of meditation will get you a step ahead so that should this seeming pain occur, you are already very skilled at getting your answers. Archangel Raphael can, when requested, come into your physical body and cleanse and heal cell by cell. Be ready for a miracle healing. Angels make them happen every day. The belief that you must endure pain is a falsehood. Do not tolerate pain at all.

A Deep and Cleansing Breath

To breathe in means to breathe in spirit. A deep and cleansing breath will allow you to breathe in spirit and breathe out the negative ions that bog you down. A deep, cleansing breath gives you an opportunity for a mini-meditation to get you centered in love again. Use this as needed throughout your day. Breathing in spirit will help cleanse you. There are many times that this is a good thing to do. For example, if your boss comes to you and criticizes your work and, hopefully, not you, too, you can take a cleansing breath which will allow a moment to organize your words. The words will then come from love and be useful and productive rather than a negative or fear-based reaction to what was said. Remember, ego is always ready with nasty retorts. You do not want these kinds of remarks associated or attached to you.

A deep and cleansing breath can be a good idea when there is a decision to be made. One clue that a cleansing breath is needed is that you will notice your body sigh. Repeat a deep and cleansing breath and if you are paying attention, you will feel the warmth that occurs inside of you whenever you breathe in spirit. Teaching this mini-meditation technique to others will help your associates to better communication. Before you speak you may ask, "What would spirit have me say in this situation?" The answer will come immediately. Remember, your goal is perfect communication and expressing love. It is not to try to put the other person down or to give them a feeling of lack or disappointment. Watch your words and you will see a difference. This technique when employed regularly can change the whole basis of relationships whether it is at work, at home, in church, or other leisure time activities.

We have told you that you are a beacon to others. They will follow your example. Do you not see how you can change the world? A deep and cleansing breath will help communication and teaching with your children. Remember, they look to you as an example of how to live. Asking spirit to help choose your words will make sure that your words are the right words that will positively teach or influence your child. You will give them a foundation that will help to build a beautiful and loving life for them. This is important. Your children chose you as a parent. You must do the right thing.

Again, let us point out that this is not difficult and the more you do it the easier and more frequent it gets. Do not judge yourself if you let an opportunity go by that you do not speak your truth. Merely notice it and plan to do the right thing the next time and then *forget it*. You may quietly say to yourself that you apologize for the remark, or you may say it in person to whom you spoke. Regardless, the use of words is important. Ask for guidance. We are here to serve you and we feel great joy when you allow us to help.

Opening your heart to love begins with a simple exercise. First, take a deep, cleansing breath. Yes, breathe in spirit. Now feel the essence inside you. It is glowing and burning brightly. As you breathe in feel this essence grow bigger and stronger. It grows until it fills your entire physical body. It continues to grow and surrounds you. You can feel the presence of God within as you start to feel love for all mankind. Yes, this is a safe and warm feeling that you enjoy. You will do this simple exercise many times throughout the day. You will do this when you feel sad, tired, lonely, overwrought, painful, weak and forgotten.

This will free you when you feel imprisoned by the tasks of your life. This will help you stay centered in love. Now that you are feeling the warmth and the love you have for others with whom you are one, you can feel the love returning to you a thousand fold as you once again breathe in a deep, cleansing breath. You are free and ready to accept love into your heart. You feel it from every direction and from every source in the universe. You are loved by all and return love to all. As you continue to go about the work and play of your day you feel lighter than air. You are walking on a cloud and nestled in the arms of your angels and God's love. God loves you and blesses you for you are sacred to Him and to your mission. You are never alone. By doing this simple exercise you can remind yourself that God is everywhere. God is a part of you. Only love is real.

Chapter 10

Life Is Fair

Equal and fair

In life one forgets one's purpose and the challenges and growth one has asked to experience in this life. Instead, one runs around screaming, "Life is not fair!" or, "It is not fair!" Or, one suggests and complains that one wants equal time and benefits with everyone else. Life *is* fair. You get what you have asked for.

As you realize now, there are many ways to ask for what you think you don't want. You may focus and worry and dread that a certain situation will occur. That is asking for it. You may exclaim, "With my luck I'll run out of gas!" or, "With my luck the gas station will be closed!" Instead, please ask your angels to direct you to the nearest open gas station and visualize yourself making it all of the way there. If this does not happen, then you have attracted the situation for a reason. You can ask yourself why, and the answer will be readily available. Perhaps the lesson is to teach you not to be so negative in your thinking and speech. That is a fair lesson to learn.

Life would not be fair if you were not getting the situations to learn the lessons you chose to learn in this life. If the lesson seems harsh or seemingly painful, remind yourself that this is what you have planned to do. Then, set about solving the problem or meeting the challenge in a very matter of fact way. Change your perspective on how you look at the bumps in your life. It is also okay to say that you are not choosing to solve any more problems today. Allow yourself time to meditate and clear the negative energy that may be attached to the situation that you are complaining about and look at things with a new, fresh attitude in the morning. We see you lie awake at night worrying and fretting. We yearn to comfort you and still your mind. When one chases elusive sleep with a burdened mind, it is time to give those problems to us. We repeat ourselves here because we shout aloud to you daily, "Ask us to help!" Remember that your life is not one lone event in time, but an interval on the continuum of the many cycles of life you have had and will continue to have.

Purpose

You came to this life to fulfill your mission. You have a purpose. All truth lies within that purpose. All is fair and equal. The pre-ordained beautiful purpose lies within you. A quiet meditation will help you focus. Notice where your footsteps have led you. Do you not see that you have walked around and around skirting the purpose? Allow these thoughts to enter. Allow us to show you what you have forgotten. This truth decides all. The walk of one's purpose is joyful and blissful. It is divinely ordained that it should be so. Each heart beats as one. All work for God. The symbolism here is unique. It points to truth and light. Even though you may not see your purpose yet, it is there and waiting. Your footsteps lead you on to discovery. Realize that you are already doing God's work of enlightenment and service. Allow the light to shine through you and from you. Be the example in your circle. Allow the feelings of joy to rain down upon you as you realize that you are on your task. This task is filled with love and joy for your fellow man. Whether it is healing, teaching or serving, you have arrived.

Feeling secure in your purpose is a familiar, warm, and friendly feeling. You really feel one with all of life and feel tremendous desire to unselfishly serve others. You attract people, animals and life forms that need your special talents and abilities. Each time you heal, teach, or serve in another way, you feel satisfied and excited and content that you are on your mission and know it. Others will come to you just as you seek and find the individuals who specialize in satisfying your needs and desires. This harmony among men is the way that God has planned it to be. Ego is forever banished from all. This harmony causes Mother Earth to sing her song of joy, health and bliss as she continues to serve all of life.

Preparation for fulfilling your life purpose began long ago. Perhaps you were led to the right school, training center and to the teachers who could mentor you for a time. All of these experiences along the way make up the background that prepares you to find and live your purpose. Fulfilling your purpose gives such joy and comfort to your soul that you feel that you have truly come home again. As others come to you, you also become a teacher. No matter what your purpose is you will also teach others the source of your happiness and love.

With desire and intent in your heart, ask your angels to show you pictures of you doing your life purpose. Ask them to show you putting your special talents and abilities to work serving others and serving the planet. You may see pictures or you may hear a voice to give you clues and words. Still, another way is to just feel that you want to follow a certain path. The angels may guide you by giving you information and you feel you just know what your mission is. You may not know how or why you know, but you do. These are all types of communication with the angelic realm and God. As you continue to serve, the angels and God will fine tune your skills to help you function at an optimum level. As you are on your purpose you will also live a life of abundance, happiness, joy and love.

Chapter 11

Conquering Challenge

Challenges

This time of life (yours and the planet Earth's) brings challenges in many guises. Some are considered easy and you meet them and solve them without even realizing that you have. You have prepared for some and maybe do not realize that you have. Others get interpreted as huge challenges and can seem to you most overwhelming. Yet we are here. We stand by to make this life easier for you. Remember to enlist our help. Long ago you promised that you would do so. We caution you to look at a seeming challenge in a new light.

First, please realize that a challenge is only a seeming problem waiting for a solution. Solutions are easy and plentiful. You have brought hundreds and thousands of solutions to problems all of your life. Give yourself credit and a pat on the back. Many seeming problems do have many solutions. Asking for angel assistance and connecting with the higher self allows you to see the big picture and choose the solution more likely to be effective as your first choice. Asking others in your life for their opinion can be helpful, but remember that no one else can get the big picture and give you a solution which is superior and perfect for all concerned.

Also, a solution needs to be perfect in all directions of time. Ask the angels to help you see, feel, know or hear the perfect solution. Sometimes, as you know, you merely give the problem to the angels and the solution will occur in a most natural manner. These coincidences, as you call them, are not at all coincidences but the actual manifestation of divine help, guidance and intervention.

Others may ask you for your advice for the solutions to their problems. Your part in this is to offer possible solutions or relate solutions that have worked for you in the past. Most importantly, your words need to guide them to go within and use the master problem solvers, the higher self, God and the angelic realm. When you go within more happens than just a solution to a seeming problem. Spiritual growth can occur and it is magnificent for you to experience. This feeling is empowering and helps you to realize that you are indeed in charge of your life. Remember, when you ask for angel assistance you do not have to follow their advice. Recording these solutions and their sources in a journal assists you to remember how successful this combination can be when working together.

The challenges of planet Earth come from her long suffering at man's hand. The burning, bombing, anger and fear that man clothes her in must end now. In this new millennium, many voices are needed to be heard by Mother Earth to soothe her, to calm her, to cleanse her, to nurture her and to allow her to heal herself. Do your part. Small kindnesses to her will always serve her well. And, do serve her well as she has sustained and served mankind for eons.

Learning

We wish to speak to you now of learning. Learning that takes place each and every day. This is why you have certain things occur in your life. The learning can undo and replace past mistakes. Learning will prevent new mistakes from occurring. When you have learned you have internalized information and made it a part of your very being. This is most precious. We smile to see how you feel when this learning occurs. Do not mix up learning for blaming yourself that something has occurred. Do not get wrapped up in blaming and cursing yourself. Instead, recognize when you have learned something and make it a part of you. This is a joyful time, a time to celebrate, because you never have to learn that lesson again. If the same situation occurs you will merely plug in the information and experience you have learned. You will see your learning in practice. Celebrate. We are joyous for you at these times, but we truly want to see you feel the same as we do. We are on your side. We cheer you on. We are your pep team.

Change

Hastening to make changes is making the easy less easy. Change can come instantaneously whenever desired. However, on your Earth plane you are not familiar with quick changes in behavior. Alas, but you are reluctant to believe in miracles happening to you. We wish to ease you into the truth that miracles with angels happen every day. You can get used to this way of doing things and running your life. Consulting with God and the angels can bring instantaneous results. Have you not wished for something to happen or for a pain to leave you to find that your wish was granted instantaneously? Yet, when you start to ponder this miracle it seems unreal and quickly becomes unreal and all is lost again and the pain has returned.

Practice with the mind to understand that the illusion can be quickly dissolved. The illusion is your seeming problem or your seeming pain. When you are used to and truly believe and understand these quick solutions, you will find that life is easier. No waiting required. Allow the angels to assist you in your new thinking pattern. Your reality which includes miracles of all sizes happens daily and frequently. Share these expectations with your brothers and sisters that they, too, will understand and accept these manifestations that can and do occur so quickly. What begins as thought becomes reality whether it is bad or good. Remember to look at this from what may be a new vantage point.

Envy

Be thankful and praise God for who you are. Do not envy another. Do not request to walk in his shoes because you do not know where those footsteps may lead you. Rejoice that you are an important part of a divine existence with your special purpose to complete. What looks appealing in the life of another may actually be a challenge or even a reward that person has asked for and is experiencing. To feel envy is to deny your love that you have for yourself. Count your successes. There are many. We know and remember them all.

Chapter 12

Healing Affirmations

Reality

Working on the reality is as you make it. Shift your gaze inward and notice the true feelings of self. There is no pain, hate, anger or dissatisfaction. There is only love. Think and plan for the optimum and perfect life. The life you have is on a mission and a purpose. The purpose is to serve. The mission may be a choice of many different fields. Teaching, healing, learning, challenging and more. The mission is yours to discover and to remember. You planned it long ago. You may have a mission which has to do with the challenges of the new millennium. You may have volunteered to help mankind and Mother Earth through this time of transition and hope. You will help heal the world.

We have spoken of healing by taking one by the hand one at a time. As we have said millions are needed now. As you pray and meditate, ask for help to heal the many angry souls around the globe, those souls who are lose and feel forgotten. It is they who have forgotten God. The power of many prayers is great and can make a huge difference in your world. The reality you have is what you make it. Should you place emphasis on negative thinking and lack of bounty that is the way you shall live. Feel and know that you are worthy and deserving of abundance. The abundance in every area of your life is waiting for you and is yours if you only think and plan that you have it. There can be an abundance of love, friends, happiness, money, and material goods to keep you comfortable every day of the rest of your life. We will teach you affirmations or perhaps you know of them already. These affirmations put all in the present tense. Here are some to try on:

* I have all the money that I need.
* My needs and wants are satisfied now.
* I have an abundance of loving friends around me now.
* Angels surround me now and assist me in every part of my life.
* I live in a comfortable, pleasing and beautiful home.
* I have leisure time for all of my desired activities now.
* My family and I enjoy perfect health, harmony and love.
* The choices I make every day are good and perfect for all concerned.
* I radiate love, warmth and kindness to all I meet every day.

Use these affirmations. Use them to manifest a reality for you. Also, use them to stimulate thinking and learning that there is an affirmation for everything you need, want and desire. Do not join in the negative thinking. It is just as easy to make a positive affirmation as it is to complain endlessly about one's lot in life. You are not a victim. You have attracted all to you. Remember the lessons to be learned and the growth to be achieved. These affirmations bring easy lessons. See the lesson, recognize, and learn from it. Incorporate the new thinking into your daily life and into your thoughts, deeds and actions. There is no need to live without abundance. That is not God's wish for you. Remember, give it to the angels to manifest for you the perfect life. Be comfortable as you continue to work your mission and fulfill your purpose.

The Certain Knowing

The certain knowing comes upon you. It is there and you notice it. You may acknowledge it as well. Do so. It is knowledge with a meaning and an indication and instruction for you. Respect it and know it is the truth and it will lead you to more knowledge and truth. It may be a quiet voice which is not speaking. The knowing brings to you a special contentment. You are very wise and wiser to listen, trust and act on this special knowingness. It pervades you and surrounds you. It is warm and comforting. It is also familiar. It is also kind. Is it scary? Only if you feel unsure that you are loved and cared for.

Know this above all things: You are loved by God and are prized by all who exist. Follow the guidance that comes to you. Depend on it. So, you say the immediate result may not be the desired one. But you know in your heart what you need and desire. This intention will bring all to you. If you do not recognize this knowing as the answer you have waited for or searched for, ask your angels to clarify and repeat. We will do so for you. We want you to know and feel and hear and see our messages for you. We will help you. Although you may see pictures that are mystifying, you can and should ask us to clarify and we will.

We so enjoy our time with you. We love and thrive on your attention to us and requesting our assistance. We are one with you and we want all good for you, maybe at times more than you do for yourself. We put you number one. Number one is where you belong and where you really are. Do you realize this? Know it for sure because it is so. We have seen your dark hours. Darker than ever we have found you at times. This is when you must call us. These familiar dark hours can easily and quickly be chased away by us and by you when you recognize your tremendous power and strength. You have the power and strength of the entire mighty universe behind you. This is awesome to you, but we know it and take it for granted that you will call on this godly strength in every hour of need. We stand here to remind you. We will make the connection for you. Accept this truth and more will follow. You are created perfect, whole and complete. Remember.

Chapter 13

Making the Right Choices

Pathways

The pathways that are chosen need to be revisited. Making choices and selecting your path must be done to help you to gain insight and to remember what you have come to do. When you have a path that forks, ask your angels to assist you in making the right decision. The angels can give you more information to allow you to make a more insightful decision. Asking the angels to help you to meditate on the future will also assist you. Meditation time can be spent doing a progression into the future to look at your life one year from now. This is the picture you will be shown of what your life will be like if you stay on the path that you are on.

Other choices come along and may change the direction you actually take. It is all up to you. You have free will to make any choices that you want. You may ask for and follow angelic guidance or not. It is up to you. There are no coincidences in your life, so each choice is an opportunity for growth or will lead you to another growth opportunity. Events will occur that help you down the path of your life's purpose. These events have been divinely arranged to speed you on your way and to make your path easier to follow. When everything seems to fall into place for you, you can be sure that divine intervention occurred to give you the opportunity to make choices for your best interest. Trust in these choices. You will soon see that you made the right decision and you will be reaping the benefits.

Opening Doors

There are many doors opening for you in your lifetime. Some of them you will enter and others you will not. Please know that when there is an ending to one phase of your life that another one is soon to be starting. This is a time of excitement and joy for you! This becomes your opportunity to continue to do your life's work or purpose. Know that we are there for you and arrange these opportunities. There is sadness and despair among you often when situations change in your life. Do not dwell on these past events. You will look at them only in terms of the growth lessons you have learned. It is time to move on.

The next journey awaits you. Leap into it with great joy and anticipation. Ask for angelic guidance. The new situation can be similar to the old situation if the growth lessons have not occurred. Ask your angels. Recognize familiarity when you see it so that you can show a change in behavior that means that you have really learned what you came here to learn and that you are ready to be involved in new situations. There is no insignificant fact in your life. All has meaning, yet we do not expect or desire for you to take every one of them and dissect them and evaluate them for meaning. For now, merely noticing is enough. Know that the information is there for you to refer to when you need it. We will nudge you along.

Destination

The destinations are of your own choosing. Know that each day you can be on your purpose or heading towards it. Many times it takes many of your Earth years to prepare. However, a life of service to others can begin early on. Finding and noticing opportunities to be helpful to others can be everyone's common goal and way of life. Merely a smile or being a good and willing listener can help. Pointing out someone's strengths can be an enormous help. At each and every opportunity you are critical to someone else's life plan. A behavior on your part that may seem insignificant to you can be important to someone else. You are not an isolated being. You are all connected. Each part of the whole works together to a common goal and purpose, that of love and service to one another and living in harmony with all other beings. A daily affirmation that, "I will be centered in love today and love will guide my actions," can start the day off right. This affirmation, whether written on paper and posted where you will frequently see it or memorized, can remind you all day long of your plan. When using these affirmations frequently you will see a change in your words and behavior. Then, you will see a difference in how you feel. You will delight at seeing that you have changed the way others feel as well. This is a simple and beautiful gift you can share with all whom you meet in a day's time. This will not be a struggle or difficult to do when you ask for angel assistance. Ask Archangel Gabriel to assist you as well. She is the archangel of communication and she will help spirit guide your words and actions.

Go with the Flow

Guiding you from here necessitates that you go with the flow! As you listen to your inner guidance and follow it, you will be an integral part of the flow of knowledge, truth and love in this universe. You are a part of God and all goes well for you. Take time to notice, appreciate and enjoy the benefits of allowing and being open to this flow. As you are at this intuitive level answers for all quests will come easily. You will trust, discover, and find every desirable avenue open to you. Ease into this life. You will be very relaxed. You will succeed in all areas of life. You will be on your purpose. You will complete your mission. Others who are a part of your mission will join you in this easy flowing of purpose and love. You will give and receive love easily and continuously throughout each and every day. You will be an unending source of love and energy for those around you. You will teach others your open secret to successful life and living. This is your chosen work and you will do it well.

Oftentimes on your sphere there is inhibition to the flow. You can start each day with a chakra clearing and balancing exercise. Chakras are the energy centers throughout your body which must be opened to allow the energy to flow. Open chakras that are clean and balanced will allow you to more easily receive divine guidance. There are many sources for these exercises and you will find and use the ones that are right for you. Do this ritual daily or twice daily, morning and evening, to keep yourself balanced and in harmony with all life. These energy centers tarnish and clog from your fears, worries, and obsessions from life on this planet. You can rectify this easily.

When you are open to the flow, the energy courses through you giving you new feelings of life and excitement. This works for you and you will depend on it always. It is up to you to make this happen. Your angels will help you and remind you to do so.

Deserving

We will tell you now that you deserve all good in your life. You are created perfect, whole and complete, and deserve all good things and experiences to come to you. These good experiences may be challenges, but when a challenge comes you truly know that you can solve it, overcome it, and move on. Know in your heart, dearest one, that we see only good for you and send you all with love. To feel undeserving means that you feel you should be punished. Again, this is ego in charge. You know what to do about that. There is no punishment. There is no price to pay. All comes from the great source which is God. Learn this and know it and teach this truth to others. So often we see you deny yourself pleasure because of this block of feeling undeserving. You are to be rewarded for all.

Chapter 14

Staying Centered in Peace and Happiness

Peace

The peace within you now is a peace that you will keep and hold dear. This peace is a product and benefit of the pure love you feel and are. This peace dwells within you as the basis for all things. One cannot entertain negative thoughts or commit negative and aggressive actions when this peace is held within. When you are coming from a basis of peace, all resolutions to problems will occur easily and will be perfection. This peace is invasive. It fills your heart and soul and is warm like the feeling of love inside you now. The peace radiates out and fills others with a calming sense of quiet and harmony.

Take time to recognize and experience this peaceful feeling every day before you set about to do your deeds. With this peace nothing can rile you, upset you, or shake the feeling of love inside you. Others will sense your calmness and want to experience it for themselves. This peace is contagious like the love. Start each day with a quiet meditation to become centered in love and feel this peace within. During the day you may delight in a brief moment of quiet to feel this feeling and ignite it and feel it grow. You will easily slide through your day with a comfort and ease you will want to repeat again and again.

Others' interactions with you will multiply the feeling many times over until you will think you cannot hold more. This feeling escapes from you and surrounds and comforts and mystifies others around you. They, too, will feel they have had a special and delightful interruption in their normal day. Nothing is worth risking this peace. You will consider all options and choose those which protect and nurture this peaceful feeling. Cement this feeling into yourself and it will not move for anything. You will value this peace above all else.

You will now teach others how to attain this joyful feeling. You will teach them that with this peace comes safety. This peace is a feature of love and one of the benefits of living pure love. It reflects a change of attitude. It is an attitude of selflessness, yet it brings tremendous happiness and joy along with it to the purveyor of this wonderful bliss. See the fruits of your efforts become mature as you spread this feeling to those near you. They hunger for this joy as have you. They do not know where to find it until they see you and their higher self recognizes you as a leader and as an example to follow. Guard your words and thoughts, dear one, as they shall belong not only to you but to others as well.

Joy and Happiness

Living the life of joy and happiness is inherent in the existence of the soul. When God made you perfect, whole and complete, he made you full of love. This love, when brought into physical form on this planet, brings with it joy and happiness. As ego comes along, he challenges those perfect feelings and tries to abolish them. Go back to your essence. Visualize it getting larger and larger. The flame is burning brightly. You can feel the warmth expand within you. Do you not feel joyful and happy at this time? The feeling will stay with you until the ego successfully focuses your mind on the seeming problems of your life here in the physical body. Do not allow this to occur. You may act as if the telephone has rung and the person calling got the wrong number. Tell ego it is calling the wrong number and that you will not allow anyone or anything to change or permeate this perfect feeling of joy and happiness.

Remember, when your joy and happiness are threatened by your illusions of problems, that this is only a bump in the road. A bump that can be ironed out and smoothed over with angel assistance. Guard and protect and honor these perfect feelings of joy and happiness that pervade you now. You will find them overtaking you time and again and more often as you practice living this concept of not tolerating other feelings.

When you see the joy and happiness seeming to be missing from the lives of those around you, you will comfort them and remind them of the perfect essence that they are. You will remind them that they needn't focus on and tolerate these negative feelings. And, do not be overtaken yourself by these feelings of others. The negative feelings of others are part of the drama that they are living on this planet in this lifetime. They know you for a reason. Perhaps for many reasons. Remind them of perfection. Take them home again to the starting place of the perfect essence. Your heart will swell from the joy this brings you both. You are an angel on this Earth at this time. Continue on.

Chapter 15

Forgiving Ourselves and Others

Forgiveness

We will teach you now a painless process to further your spiritual evolution. You have asked for this though you do not associate it with the word forgiveness. You will leave behind debris you have accumulated for eons and ages through many lives. You have added more in this life, dear one, and we seek to assist you to cleanse and to release.

We have seen you react even in minute ways to criticism or seeming hardships brought to you by others. We see you feel the pain of a contact. We have seen the love shine less brightly when you see, meet or think of certain others you have known. And yet the seeming pain you feel will all be cleansed away today, now, and you will repeat this new habit frequently and briefly as you continue your travels on the road of knowing and living. Yes, it is to forgive others' seeming attacks on you. Yes, this is to be done. No, you do not attach these moments to your soul any longer. You can forgive and release the other party. You can look at the behavior, words, deeds and actions of others differently now. You know the source of their remarks and actions.

We are speaking of ego and speaking of the tough exterior shell one can wear. These are false fronts of your loved ones, friends, associates, co-workers and even, perhaps, the clerk at the department store. You have felt slighted, insulted, criticized, blamed and punished. You yearn to cry out, "This is not fair! I didn't do it!" and yet you swallow these words and they leave a dark spot on your soul. Knowing the source of these dark spots can make it easier to wash them away. To name the person and state your forgiveness and that you release them from any negative thought from you is to cleanse your soul and to also send love to them at the same time.

We want you to know, dearest one, that forgiveness is at the base of many issues. We ask that you feel intent and desire in your heart to truly, completely, and honestly forgive all others. Do this now. Every day at day's end you will remember your day. At this time please forgive all who must be forgiven to grant yourself peace. We tell you of another soul whom you have had great expectations. You have expected this one to be perfect in all areas. You have judged frequently and found this one lacking in many ways. Ego has jumped in and stricken with mighty punishment and harsh words which are a blow to thy heart. We speak of you, beloved, at this time. You have held yourself at too hard a task. You set the goals too high and you have too many. Ease up. Forgive yourself as you know that you, too, have ego and an outer shell to deal with. As you strip away this shell and allow ego less and less time and room to rule you, the ability to forgive yourself will come. It can come now. We stand here ready to assist you. With intent and desire in your heart ask for our help. Let us know that you are willing to release the blocks and fears you seemingly have to forgiveness.

There are those fears that seem to grab and hold you. Fears that forgiving yourself and others can only leave you feeling defeated again. This is not so, dear one. Forgiveness is the perfect solution for all because it does release everyone in all directions of time. Being burdened by unforgiveness is like being under a wool blanket in the desert. Throw it off! Throw off this burden. It does no one any good. It is a game that ego uses to keep you feeling separate from others. You know that as one, you have only love for self and all others. There is no room for unforgiveness where love reigns. We await your request. We are ready now. You will be free. You will feel love and joy bursting your heart open as you complete this cleansing of the soul.

Guilt

The time goes by quickly and we see you forlorn and fretting. This is your guilt over actions or words. Is this self-imposed or a reaction from words of another? It does not matter, dear one, for there is no reason to make guilt a part of your reality. Guilt is an illusion brought about by ego. Do not let ego torment you in this way. What is done is done and needs forgiveness and acceptance. You may truly forgive yourself if there is an action that you feel requires that, but do not allow another to bring these feelings about in you. These feelings do not lead to happiness. They lead to self-destruction. Remember that mistakes only need to be corrected not punished. Guilt is the famous punishment you bring on yourselves and freely give to others. Wipe the slate clean and remember that judgment which leads to guilt is the ego's plaything. Guilt does not come from love. Love will abolish guilt. Love yourself deeply as you truly do from the essence which is you and which is only pure love. Guilt comes from feelings of "should" and "should not." These words are different from your words and actions coming from the intent and desire in your heart.

Remember to allow others their paths full of challenges and sometimes mistakes. Perhaps it is not for you to step in to their life at that moment. Perhaps they must stand alone and use their inner wisdom which is God and the universal knowledge to solve their seeming problems. Do not take assignments from others for work which is not yours to do. If you do, you are not truly serving mankind. Guilt is a distraction sponsored and controlled by ego to keep you busy so that you do not hear your divine guidance. When you are feeling ridden with guilt and feeling badly at that, realize that ego is doing this and you know how to put him out of work. Your angels will help.

Compassion

Compassion for others and their seeming problems is an aspect of spiritual growth for all to experience and feel. As you reach out to another person, you can feel in your heart the joy and relief that one has when one is successfully facing a challenge and overcoming it successfully. To pity is not the same, dear one, for with compassion you feel in your heart the seeming struggle they face. You must cheer them on. Remind them that they have God and the angels to help them succeed. You may be a critical player in their drama at that moment. Show them the way. Speak your truth. To merely nod one's head and agree that their seeming problem is horrible only magnifies the illusion and makes it seem more real. It becomes a mountain which one might think one cannot master.

To volunteer to assist them is even better as you are an Earth angel, too. You have volunteered to come to the aid of others, always remembering that each one has his challenges coupled with a growth lesson to be learned. Soon these challenges will be overcome and they will no longer look like challenges but will be seen as opportunities to serve others. This brings great joy and lights the fire of the essence even stronger and brighter. To solve the problem is meaningless unless growth has occurred. Realize this for yourself so that you can teach this to others.

A review of the situation done in a matter-of-fact way will focus attention on the growth potential involved so that one can conquer all and grow. These opportunities to assist others abound. Remember, these situations are attracted to you and by you for your personal growth as well. There is always a lesson. To help another remove the anger, frustration, denial and fright from the situation is a service to him. He can then see clearly and not feel overpowered by the seeming problem. It is then a size that one feels one can handle. Speak your truth and show the other that the angels stand ready to assist. Show him that he knows the answers within himself and has only to stop, listen, and hear or feel the answers. Many will cross your path with their seeming burdens. You will give them the right nudge to spur them on. You will give them hope. This is a great gift all by itself.

Chapter 16

The Light

The light burns brightly and it burns for you. That white light which is God's perfect essence. It welcomes you and nourishes you and you feel as if you've come home again. Come home again. You will for the light is always there, always present and always welcoming. In the deepest of your sleep your soul returns to be rejuvenated and recharged by the light. You awaken ready to do God's work. You are his messenger to others. You are to awaken the sleeping ones and call them to duty. They, too, shall come home again. The light which is God is the divine creator of all. The all-knowing wisdom resides here in the light. As you cross the winding and treacherous path, God is with you. You have only to think of the light and you will be with Him for He is with you always. He guides and lights your way. He cradles you in his arms of love and gentle kindness.

Your soul is warmed by the light which is ever present. The journey of the soul is within this light. Though you may feel that you have passed through shadows, the light burns brightly for you. Reach out and take the hand of the Master for He shall guide you and show you the way. Return to Him and feel the oneness you have with God, the angels and all creation. This is the most beautiful of all. As you go down the path of your life and your purpose, know that He is with you always. He never leaves you to walk alone. Though He may seem lost from sight, adjust your gaze and you will see Him and know Him again and always. This is the source of your divine guidance. This is the source of your essence. This is the source of your life, the source of energy and strength. He will never fail you.

Though you may feel confused or abandoned at times, you only have to ask for his presence and you will once again be home in his ever-loving arms. Fear will melt away as if it never existed when you ask for God to rescue you from the darkness. Remember this above all else: God is with you and there is no way you can leave his presence. Even though you may feel angered and convinced that God has dealt you a terrible blow, rest easy and know that all is for the greater good and you will forever be comforted by his love.

Others have written and told the story of "the light." In their "near death" stories they speak of traveling toward the bright beautiful light which is so alluring and comforting to them. They yearn to go to the light and stay with the light. The story continues with the person being told, "Not now. You must return." They then find themselves back in their bodies and frequently their lives are changed by the experience.

Behold the light. We want you to understand and know and remember that this light is always available to you to see, feel and use. There is no need to have a "near death experience" to see and feel the power of the light. We have told you that we use many methods to awaken you and to point out certain information to you. We have many ways of communicating our messages and suggestions to you. This is a dramatic and intense way to capture your attention and trigger a life-changing event, the event you have asked for and planned to have occur in this life.

As we say, the light is always with you. It is always available. The light is the essence of God and we have spoken many times of the omnipresence of God. The person with the near death experience involving the light frequently has his or her life changed by that event. He or she probably becomes more spiritual. Sometimes it takes a major event like this to turn one around and get one on the proper path. Some of you resist the truth. You all have work to do. You all have a role.

We tell you this light is always with you. In other parts of this book we have shown you the essence which is you and have taught you how to feel and expand this essence. You may do this at any time. As you feel the essence expand and grow warmer, realize this is the same essence as the light. If you become in awe of this light know also that it is God within you. This is the same light with the same power of love that others talk about. You must seek this out and experience it completely without the drastic situation of a near death experience.

As you read of others feeling the dynamic presence of the light, you must believe that you can capture this experience for your own any moment of any day of your life. Again, we want you to experience this over and over so that more and more of you live a transformed spiritual life that keeps you on the path of love and teaching others. Share this with others. They long to remember this truth as have you. At any time that you wish you may feel the presence of the light. If you have seeming difficulty getting there, ask us to help you. Say, "I am willing to release the blocks that keep me from enjoying the light and my true essence." Immediately we will be with you and take these blocks and fears to the light. God is love. You are love. You are one and the same. Remember this and live this truth.

Chapter 17

Work and Play

Laughing and Playing

Dear one, we have spoken to you of duties, missions and your purpose. Yes, you are on your path and we wish you to understand our delight when we see you relax, play, laugh and take good care of yourself. All must balance and flow freely within you and around you.

Laughter is a tonic to renew your energy and to release the negative ions and feelings. Laughter washes over you like a fountain of love. Yes, it is nice to know that you are in balance and that you realize that life is fun. All life can be filled with joy. You may ask your angels at any time to release the blocks that keep you from experiencing true joy and bliss. Archangel Michael will come at the call of his name to release these blocks for you also. Joining with others into the sport of relaxation calms, soothes and brings you closer. These playtimes help you to remember that life isn't always work or challenges.

You deserve an intermission. Taking relaxation and respite outdoors fuels the fire of the burning essence within. Yes, we want you to hug a tree or run your fingers over the leaves of a plant. Take quiet solitude and converse with the plant fairies. Encourage them in their work as well. Tending the plants on Mother Earth is play and joy to them. Bring something from nature into your homes—flowers, plants and beautiful wood. Allow the fresh air to circulate whenever possible. Running games stimulate the euphoric feelings of love and joy. Quiet games unite the players and strengthen the bonds. As you play more and realize more and more every day how life's "work" can be fun and joyous, you will more and more delight in each and every day of your life. Teach this to others. You must spread the word. Sometimes all it requires is changing your mind and deciding that what was previously thought of as work is now fun. It is done with love and when you add love the magic happens!

Work

We speak to you of your chosen work. Finding your purpose or remembering it, as we say, is frequently deemed by you to be difficult. Yet, we can steer you in the right direction and already are doing so. Look around you at the people you see and come in contact with daily. These are your family members, your extended family of brothers and sisters whom you see at work and away. What are their needs? What problems present themselves to you through these people? Look into their eyes and see and feel the challenges they face. There may be new ones every day, but there will be many that repeat themselves frequently. These are the situations we wish for you to affect. These are the reasons others are in your life.

You have had special training between lives to do your work here on the planet. You are qualified. Remember, you are perfect, whole and complete, and very capable of affecting a change in your life and in the lives of others. Contemplate the other's situation. Ask the higher self for help and to connect with the higher self of the other person. Remember to guard against ego taking control. If your suggestions or remarks come quickly be suspect that ego is in charge. It is okay to meditate and pray for a time before you act. The more you meditate the more quickly the higher self information and the information from the angelic realm will come through. Also, you will get very adept at knowing when the information is reliable and not from ego. Also, you can get to a point where you will be verbally channeling our words directly to someone.

Look around you at your workplace. Consider that you perform certain tasks there but it really isn't "work." God has given you all of the skills to carry on these tasks. The depth of the job you are doing is more or less intense problem solving for yourself and others. You know how to do this. Remember, serving others is not work, but a joyous collection of solutions you are putting into action. As you see the effect of these solutions on those around you, you will feel less like you are "working" and more like you are accomplishing your joyous purpose mission after mission. You will know that you are completing the cycle of training, learning and serving that you started before you came to this life. You will be satisfied and anxious to repeat the process. Remember that you are one light and many are doing the same.

Vibration of the Music

We wish for you to slow down and get in tune with the music of the new millennium. The music vibrates at the frequency of the love. Hear the beat and feel the rhythm as it shows you the way the energy flows. We speak of the music that sends you to the alpha level and brings you alive with feelings of love for fellow man, Mother Earth and all of her inhabitants. This is music which came from the Pleiades when that planet became complete. These vibrations are to unite you and to help you realize that you are all one. This music gives you the opportunity to have the love within you expand and spread out without your feeling any inhibition. You cannot quell this love. You will feel it overtake you and you will feel powerless to resist the feelings, emotions and the joyful bliss this beat starts.

This music is as the call of ancient times when souls were united—souls a great distance away from each other. The united humanity has a life and existence of its own. You are all one people with one God and one existence. The work of united humanity is to heal the Earth, heal each member and teach others. In the future, you will be called on to help others who are not with you now. The unification has been planned for eons and when the parts of the whole separated you have yearned to reunify. The sound and beat of the music is a call to duty for you all to remember your purpose. You are awakening now.

Many times when words and actions do not rouse your fellow man the music will. The music awakens the memory. This memory is of the truths that govern your lives. The makers of the music are fulfilling their purpose. They are lightworkers who volunteered to help in this way. The young people will guide you to the music. Watch them and see that they live in a pure existence of love. Open your eyes, ears and hearts to the music and you will release blocks. Balance and cleanse your chakras at the same time. The music is love and only love is real. Play this music in your home. You will find it to be wonderful background music when you meditate and talk to God. Calling the angels to your side for assistance will be enhanced when the music plays. As you are immersed in the joyful music you will be more productive. Problems will seem insignificant and easily solved. Friendships will deepen. Romance will blossom. Children will feel as if they have come home. God is with you and the music tells you this. It is God's cry of love to you.

Chapter 18

Women and Children

Women

At this time we speak to you of the nurturers of your planet. They are both male and female and we shall now speak of those predominantly female. You have come to this Earth for many reasons. You are here now at a critical time. You are each very important to one another and to the whole. No one is excluded. All belong. All are deserving. Some of you have and will carry the seed to continue the growth of humankind. You will nurture each child to grow straight and tall. This is your primary purpose. All else comes along next. Those who do not carry the seed are also the teachers and nurturers of the prodigy. The united effort of creating the environment for the physical body, the soul and spirit to grow and thrive are all important. Remember that the child looks up and sees all. The child will see past the mask and know your true self.

The women come with preparations and plans to calm the waters of the struggling Earth. You know peace and can bring peace to any situation. Peace is your innermost desire. Throughout time, woman has been strong with a strength of her own that comes from the source perfect and complete. Your purpose is to bring all situations back to a love base. Yes, you are powerful, almost magical as you weave your spell of peace and love. All will listen for you are the revered woman. Know this truth. Be a shining example and others will come to you for guidance, love, and lessons. Reach out your hands and embrace all of life and all of humanity. Hold them close to your heart as all are dear to God and, thus, to you. You do not fear taking a chance. You know your own power. Ego will try to distract you, but you are steadfast on your purpose. You are the one with the knowledge and you know the ways. You are naturally organizers and you get things done. You can see the big picture in all situations.

You speak reasonably to others and can explain the truths. You can interpret these truths and teach others how to apply them. This is your special ability from God. You receive guidance from the divine easily and frequently. Your station is always tuned to the divine. You cannot stop this influx of information, energy and love. It comes to you for a reason. You are to be the transmitter of this information to others. In your dreams you learn of this love. You learn of your purposes and, yes, you have many, dear one. You are to take action and take it now. Focus your strength and all of your powers and use it now to change the lives of yourself, others, and all of humankind. You will change the course of the Earth and the destiny of all.

Do not surrender to ego who seeks and easily finds excuses for you to do otherwise. Know this is a mandate from God and we beseech you to follow it now. You are women united and on the move. This is your destiny, purpose and mission. We are with you as you go and only a prayer away. Your hand is in the hand of many angels who guide you and support you. We whisper in your ear and you know that you are not alone in this challenging, yet easy life you are living. Remember the source and remember your power.

Children

Dear one, we wish to let you know something about the children who are with you now. These children have among them many volunteers who chose to come to the Earth at this time to assist with changes in the new millennium. These children are children of truth. Many are old souls with much spiritual wisdom. As these children are nurtured and encouraged, they will blossom young and make significant contributions to humanity and to the Earth. Recognize them by their curiosity, the love in their eyes and the ease in which they help others. Yes, you will see this in the youngest of children.

Now, dear one, know that these children have chosen you to be their guides and teachers. You certainly may have old issues to work through and this you will do. Know that every child comes with a prior agreement with you to be of mutual benefit in this life. Some of these children will fulfill their missions early and depart. Do not mourn for them long, but celebrate the mastery of the challenge they have overcome. The ones who stay and grow old on your sphere will contribute much. You will be their teachers and your relationships will evolve and you will realize that they have much to teach you also. Do not think of these old souls in tiny bodies as helpless. They are not. They are very powerful beings who will contribute much.

You will begin to notice the changes occurring in the population of young people. Love comes naturally to them and you see it because they remember the truth. They are not overwhelmed with life and challenges to the extent of many older people and the love comes fresh from the source. These young people are in truth wise old souls who merely want to remind you of the love within and the oneness of all. You will recognize these people as you will look at their faces and see no mask, only love abundant and love to share. These loving beings will inspire you. They are uninhibited in sharing and showing their love. They live in complete happiness which radiates from their essence and you can mimic them and learn their truths as well. They vibrate at a level of love which will penetrate to your soul and unite you with them. They live simply and entertain no complications and their paths are predestined. Do you live with one of these souls? Look into their faces and you will know. Be ready for what you might see. They are a mirror for you to look into yourself and feel the love and joy you also hold and that you also can share.

Many changes are coming and many have come to assist in the transition. You are surrounded by loving beings on every level of existence and together we will change the world. God blesses you for your devotion to good and to love.

Animals

Animals are the joy and love embodied to assist you in this lifetime. They will absorb your negative energies, feelings and concerns. They will transfer them to God who will change them to perfect love and return them to the animal and back to you. It is instantaneous. When you look into the eyes of your pets, you will see the complete love in their souls as they fulfill their mission to bring you happiness and balance back into your life. God has sent them to you. God has made them perfect, whole and complete as He has you. Revere these messengers from God. Treat them well. Make their lives content and happy. It is so easy to do. Give them your time and give them your love. They will ease your seeming pain. They will bring balance back into your day. Look into their eyes and realize and appreciate the tremendous job that they do for you each and every day upon request. They stand ready to serve you in their own special way.

Bring these animals into your life. The higher self will help you select the right one. All wait eagerly to be adopted into your family. Do not let these wonderful loving souls perish. There aren't really enough to go around. Seek an animal to bring this joy to you. God has created solutions in great abundance. These solutions abound to rectify and solve your seeming problems. Know that a few minutes spent in quiet kindness to an animal are worth a half-hour of meditation time. Communicate with the animal. See and feel and appreciate his existence of pure love. This love is for you and there is plenty more to come. Plenty more to spread around as this pet shares his loving being with you and yours. Respect this perfect child of God for he is very, very special and has an important role on this Earth.

Go to your animal shelters and bring home a new friend. He will soak up your love and affection and return it a thousand fold when it may seem that no one else on Earth has a moment or a kind word for you. Feed him, groom him and take good care of his physical palace that he may stay content and serve you all of his days. God has blessed the animals for they are special.

Chapter 19

Mother Earth

True Vision

As the eye scans the land searching for a beautiful sight, the mind also roams searching for beauty, comfort, pleasure and love. All is God and God is a part of all. God is one with the trees, the land, the living beings, animals, and all that is Mother Earth. We ask you now, precious one, to see the beauty of God everywhere and in everyone. We have spoken words to you to remind you that all are your brothers and sisters on this Earth and the many other levels of being. As you see the beauty of the sloping mountain range, see the beauty of God in your fellow man. Each is created differently and yet all are the same. All are one. You and all others are one with Mother Earth. Yet, we see her mistreated by the many human parts of her great being, the bombs, the fires, the gouging of the forests and the pollution of her seas.

This is a dark spot on her aura and in her very essence. It will take man and many Earth beings and help from our sister planets to right the wrongs done to Mother Earth. She cries and beseeches you to change your ways. Where she is tended with love she rejoices and takes care of all. She provides a home for each and every one of you. See that you are in truth one with her as she is one with God and all of creation. Know that you must include her well being in your prayers and in your thoughts and deeds. Teach each and every one of your brothers and sisters to notice and realize that it is time to correct the past mistakes. This will change the path that she is on and where Mother Earth is headed. We have spoken to you of your power. Use that magnificent and awesome power to take care of this supreme being, Mother Earth. We thank you.

Encouragement

We wish to show you, beloved, and thank you for your good deeds and kind help. We see you living truly as you are one with God and the angels. We see and feel your many kindnesses every day to your brothers and sisters and all around you on our Earth. We see and feel you may be physically worn and weary, and yet you summon strength from within and perhaps from us as well and take steps to help or to serve another.

Although from time to time you have done "thankless jobs" in truth they are not. The interaction between two is never thankless. Through and because of the weariness in another you may not get a thank you in spoken words. Realize, though, that the kindness you have done in service to others gets relayed from them to others yet. We feel your gentle touch as you caress and quiet the fussy infant. We see your love radiate as you help a wounded animal. The love and excitement in your being as you tend your spring garden is thank you to us.

We appreciate your tending to Mother Earth. Your selflessness we see when you pray for others who need God's help touches us dearly and we are so proud. You solve problems and challenges every day and so much you search for solutions perfect for all. We are happy to assist and to help you on your path in service to others. You show patience in teaching the children who yearn for more and more knowledge and yearn for the wisdom you have to share. Like wild mushrooms, the children grow rapidly and spread their special love to those around them. Blessed are the patient and kind teachers who guide our children. The work of the world that requires muscle and physical strength is precious to your progress on your sphere. You build highways for travel and this brings faraway brothers and sisters closer. The farmer who tills the soil to feed the many is given a thank you as you nourish the physical bodies which are the homes for the souls. A star shines in the sky for every act of kindness you each have done. As you look at the night sky, see these reminders that you are on your proper paths doing your special work and executing your special plans and goals. Know that you do them well and that we love you unconditionally. We are exhilarated to be a part of your lives and await your call for our assistance.

Hope

We talk to you now of hope. Hope for you as a part of the wholeness with God and as part of the universe and a member of the planet. All can be lost except hope. We see the situations and seeming challenges you face. Losing the life of a dear one near to you. We see the seeming strife you endure hanging on to feelings of hope. You hope for and wish for a greater power to bring perfect solutions. We tell you now, dear one, that there is a greater power. This is the power of God and the angels who are one with you. God is everywhere as we have taught you and you remember this truth. We are teaching you to channel these feelings of fear which give rise to feelings of hope that you can effect an outcome merely by calling on God and the angels to come to your side. Give permission for us to intercede in your behalf and on the behalf of all involved.

Hope is a feeling but a feeling of inaction. Taking action and turning hope into a perfect outcome occurs with God's intervention. Remember, there is a divine plan and each soul fulfills his own destiny even though he can change that destiny at any time by making different choices. Each person comes to fulfill his plan of challenges and accomplishments. Each person is on a mission and has a purpose. As you hope and pray ask for the perfect solution. Ask for the releasement of fears that block these perfect solutions in your life. Yes, God sees and feels your hopes and your prayers. He acts on your behalf.

Remember, life is fair and the solutions that come are not only perfect, but appropriate for you. As you feel this hopefulness that you turn into action, realize the lessons to be learned at this time. Meditate, contemplate and ask for divine guidance. Feel and internalize the new information or old information that is being repeated and know the warmth that comes with true learning and true spiritual growth. With this knowing comes comfort no matter what the situation. A comfort that God is with you and He is comforting all who seek Him. This spiritual growth that has happened took action on your part. You will want to repeat this and obtain that wonderful feeling of advancement again. You are rewarded. This is part of what you came here to do. There will be more. Use this new growth and knowledge to teach and to serve others. Then the circle and cycle is complete. You are an integral part of the whole and sometimes it is your turn to act and make a difference. Make it in a positive way. As you help mankind, so do you help Mother Earth.

Chapter 20

Help On Call

The Mirror Image

The mirror image is a reflection of you. The faces you see and the people you greet are your teachers. They teach you in their words, deeds and actions. Frequently you have an eye for knowing that the lesson is in progress. Yes, and often you choose to disregard the lesson. It will only be presented to you again and again, dear one. This you know, too, for a failure to learn is only a mistake and you shall be given more opportunities to learn. Also, there are opportunities to practice, to try on new ideas and old habits to see how they feel, and to see how you feel wearing the garb. These signs of learning will be present. You will see the earnest gaze your mirror person has. The gaze will light a spark of interest and perhaps intrigue in you as you excitedly wait to see what is next.

Do not be disappointed as we see you are sometimes. This is opportunity knocking. It is an opportunity for you and your partner in this venture to learn. It is an opportunity to act out and express the love of oneness which you share. No, you may not realize this is what is happening, but we tell you now that nothing is by chance and no interaction is insignificant. You make a difference. You matter. You count. You are important. You are the teacher. You are the student. There is no difference in status or elevation between student and teacher. One is not better than the other. All are equal. The one who realizes that this opportunity is an opportunity may be the wiser, but perhaps only this time. Experience the lesson. Give and teach. Show appreciation. Sometimes you say on your plane "This is cool." Repeat that now to the other. He will instantly recognize and know your meaning. He will share your feelings. He will at some level agree. You are on your path. You are on your purpose.

The mirror image can also reflect to you the way that you may be addressing life or problems at this time. Do not ask why everyone is angry today, but ask why you are angry today and many people needed to point that out to you. You are not focused and so we give you these reminders or points to focus on for a reason. You understand this. The work of clearing the anger or problem begins at home. It begins with you, does it not? You shall ask for our help. The first step of realizing the mirror shows yourself is the greatest step you can take on the path to fully becoming your true self, to be the living example of love on this planet. If the mirror is cloudy and you cannot see you may cleanse it by meditation, asking angels for help, talking to God and doing a chakra clearing exercise to fine tune and open your communication channels with the divine.

You are never alone. You never face a seeming problem or seeming crisis alone. We are all here as we have promised you and have shown you many times. Do not forget us. We anxiously await the precious song we hear as your voice calls to us for help.

Help on Call

The help you need is available at every turn. We are here and we are with you. You also have help you can see more clearly. This help may come from a neighbor, a friend, a stranger with a smiling face or from someone whom you least expect. These special people have volunteered to come to the planet at this time of great need. They are here to relieve stress and anger and fear on the planet. These wonderful people want to relieve the small stresses that you acquire daily. These small stresses can seemingly drain you and tire you out. This interferes with the love essence which yearns to glow bigger and brighter. The friendly clerk, the helpful receptionist, the young carryout person at the grocery store help to ease your stress. When someone smiles and says "hello," realize that this is a gift from your brother or sister to ease your day. Focus on their words and face and feel the warmth come over you in a joyous and familiar way.

These are voices meant to reach to your very soul to encourage you, to love you and to cheer you on your way. You, too, have come for this purpose and you, too, can be the friendly, smiling face to another. The smile and the kind words send energy, yes, energy to you to spur you on and to raise your mood. Feel this golden energy coursing through your soul and your body as you realize that you can make it through the day and that you are not alone. There are many who care. Look for them. See them and thank them. You can in turn send that energy to another and light his way. God loves you and God blesses you for this gift you share. You are healing the planet with your kindness and love.

Chapter 21

A Message from Archangel Michael

The Power of Love

Love is pure. In its pure form it is a magical and simple essence. The essence is a seed inside you which you can nurture and grow. The nurtured seed will grow and expand and like the growing oak tree will branch out touching many. The simple and pure love of God is God and compels all to return that love to Him.

The feeling of love does many things. It cancels and abolishes the pain. The pain of simple matters experienced on this planet. The pure love overrides feelings of envy, jealousy, anger and hate. Love has power. Love is power. Use this power to enhance your life and to enhance and to save lives and souls of others. Reach out with the love to heal others. Heal yourself. It is this pure love that makes you perfect, whole and complete. Love is joyous. Love in its simple and pure form encompasses all and melts away the tiredness and feelings of worthlessness.

You are important to God. It is important to God and the angels that you are comfortable, content and joyous and rewarded as you continue to do your life mission or purpose. These rewards stem from the love essence burning inside of you now. The expansion of that essence or flame attracts more love and joy to you. It is like a magnet. Remember that you are a beacon to draw others to you. Others will come to you to bask in the light and warmth of your love. They will sense and feel your joy. Others will come to hope for a miracle by your mere presence.

Others will come to see if you are real. And still others may come to taunt you. You will not be angered or saddened by this. You will welcome it as an opportunity to shine your essence brighter and welcome a forlorn soul who has forgotten all.

As your essence burns brighter it nurtures itself by the presence of love and good deeds, loving deeds. Love brings joy and this joy can and will overcome much. You will no longer see and be fooled by the thick shell your sisters and brothers have. Your gaze will penetrate to their very essence and being and it will fan their flame, too, so it may also burn brighter. You will see the need and desire in their eyes and you will hear it in their words. You will recognize the fears that seem to have a hold on them now and you will heal them by thinking and expressing pure love.

Pure love means safety for all who feel it. You are all safe and God has promised and shown you that is true. Hold the hand of thy neighbor that you shall lead him into more beautiful days and times. Your actions will stimulate others' acts of kindness, gentleness, and love. Each day holds new promises of adventures in love and loving for you. An argument that does not happen. An accident that does not occur. Money that arrives. New friendships that are formed. Old friendships that are eased and renewed. These are the benefits of love. Oh, yes, you know that there are many more. It is only to live and be that you shall see and feel them. All around you the magic of love is working everywhere all of the time. You see it in the children as they play. They are carefree and feel safe and loved and joyous as they play with one another. This child within which is you feels the same way. You have attracted only good, meaningful and positive energies into your life.

The challenges of your life still come. You look at them differently now. These are delightful problems that do not weigh you down, but prompt your loving actions to secure a solution which is beneficial to all. Each problem solved brings more and more joy. Give it away. You cannot use it up. The more you give love the more you get back. Use this love also to heal the Earth. She is wounded and needs your loving help to survive. Purify, cleanse and caress her where you live. Clean her, comb her, and groom her to beautiful perfection. The plant angels will help. Small beings will delight in your plan and activities. All will be well and she will smile again and sing a gentle tune. Send your love and joy around the world. Send it again and again. The more you send it the more who will benefit and will catch this contagious feeling of joy, love and safety. Needs and wants will become their reality that is met easily and perfectly by God and the angels.

There is much fear and darkness on the Earth right now. Do not hold back. Spread the love enthusiastically and you will have recruited your family, friends and neighbors to a healing beautiful army of action multiplied by the thousands and the millions as you all join together in a common goal. One can lose all, but one will never lose love. If you think you have lost love, please continue to look inside you because it is still there waiting and hungering for your acknowledgement to fan it brighter and brighter. Love is the tonic for fatigue. Love is the answer to problems. Love is the warrior who banishes anger and hate. Love is the welcome at the harbor for the lost. Love is in exchange for uncertainty and fear. Love holds a bright candle for all who feel in the dark.

This is your essence. This is what you have. This is you. This is everyone on your planet. Yes, the darker the soul or the worse the action, the more the love is needed to be felt and nurtured and acknowledged. Be the answer. You are the answer. You are one answer and millions are needed now. Rejoice that you are here at a special time and that you have volunteered to do this work. It is work that is really an act of love repeated many times. God bless you.

Afterword

The Ancients

The wisdom of the ancient dwellers on your planet has been handed down through many ages and many lifetimes. This wisdom came with them from God as rules and truths. These truths we have asked you to remember. At this time you can turn to many for their wisdom and you can remember to turn inward to your higher self for the same. You do hold all past, present and future information in your auric field and in the higher self. You have access to all wisdom.

As you go about your daily lives call upon this source of knowledge, wisdom and answers to guide your steps, choices and decisions. You shall not go wrong. Recognizing ego's attempts to intervene is important. You have now released the blocks to living as one with God and others on your sphere. You have come a long way and now you are indeed an ancient yourself. Share this wisdom with others as they do not evolve as rapidly as you have. You have reached out for the knowledge and guidance in these pages and you have benefited from the words. You will also share this information. This is not new information for you. You recognize it and remember it, do you not?

Trust in these words as you trust in God. You must also trust the process of life. All comes full circle. All is meaningful and important. Remember that there are no accidents and all is brought to you because you have requested it. Your natural desire is to grow, learn and evolve. You will do it with the strength of the higher self, God, the angels and the ascended masters. All are ready to assist you in any way. You may lean on them yet still be tall and strong. Many tall trees make up the forest and all are connected. The universe is a vast and wonderful place to exist. There is much traveling between planets and spheres. You have many cousins in this universe and many have come to help the Earth at this time. Look for these souls from beyond your Earth's limits and thank them for their special help. All working together will create a new millennium of happiness, joy, peaceful existence and the reality of love.

Conclusion

I have given you examples of walking, talking, and living love. I speak of the Ascended Masters. Many have walked the Earth. You look up to them and worship them and know their special lives are lived to give you freedom and guidance. This I have done. Do not put them above yourselves. This puts them out of reach in your lives. This is not so. In an inkling you may also live and be a master. You can decide in this present moment that you will live henceforth as did Jesus or any other. When you live in love and act in love, you have renounced that which is evil. You will teach others. You will know there is no other way to live. Pray to me and I shall grant these requests.

It is only your reality which needs to change from illusion to reality. You may return to be that which I created at any time. Let go of the illusions you hold which are not love. All else is to go by the way. You may ask for your lessons to be condensed into one time fragment which will evolve you rapidly. The angels I have sent to you will help you. You can hear my voice at any time. You can feel my love at any time. It will not cease to exist. It is the truth. Fly to Me now. You are under my wings. You can change the destiny of your world. Do not seek answers elsewhere. Go within and into Me for your guidance and lessons. Go within for my love which is always a part of you.

Love thy neighbor all your days as if he is Me. I am there wherever your gaze rests. I am with you always. The poor shall cease to be poor. The unwise will become wise. The unable will remember they are whole. Justice will be eliminated as you see that your mistakes need only correction. The ill will breathe new life into themselves, a life that comes from Me and shall last through all time and creation. Know my voice, my hand, my walk and my love that you shall return whole to Me and share my days forever.

Within these pages you have seen and felt our guidance and our love. I speak of the angels and the others who assist Me to provide for your well being and progress through your evolution. The love in these pages is meant to warm you, to move you and to make you think in new ways or to help you to remember the old ways. Guidance from us is always available and ongoing. We reach out to you constantly. We wait for you to hold the extended hand as part of your life. I say to you that daily communication with Me is what I desire. Contact Me and speak to Me at any time. Speak to Me when you have need. Speak to Me when you feel full to over-flowing with love for all. Speak to Me when you feel pride. Speak to Me when you have accepted help and are satisfied and full of joy.

Your earthly troubles are also spiritual conquests to be made. You are strong. You know that you are perfect, whole and complete. I have said this to you and this is how I have made you in my image. Gather your thoughts, pray for good for all mankind, for the Earth and all of her inhabitants. As these days and months and years on your calendar unfold, you will see that you are making progress in many ways. You will feel the shining that comes from within as you discover, feel and live in perfect joy, love and happiness. My angels depend on you to call them and they await your requests. Take a moment to thank them afterwards as it is their only pay and they delight in knowing that they have helped bring you more joy.

You have much to do. Remember, it is easy and it is fun. It is joyous to serve others and you have experienced this and know it is true. I ask you to remember to speak your truth. Speak of love, kindness and good deeds. The ego will pass away and you will truly feel and know that you are perfect, whole and complete. Joyous times are ahead and there is much splendor coming. First, take care of Mother Earth, your sisters and brothers, and all of those who cohabit this planet with you. The cycle is only complete when every link has joined the whole. My heart and love are with you each and every one at all times. You deserve this and it is so. I bless you all as you go onward on your journeys of love.

About the Authors

Sharon Rahm, R.N., and her sister, Wendy Krause, are Certified Spiritual Counselors, certified by the American Board of Hypnotherapy. Sharon and Wendy are Lightworkers and work with their clients to receive and give messages from the Angelic Realm. Through a one-on-one session, classroom setting, or lecture, Sharon and Wendy teach their clients how to communicate with the angels to seek assistance from these loving, powerful messengers of God. Sharon and Wendy reside in Arizona and you can visit them on their website at www.angelsisters.com.